PRAISE FOR *AND GOD SAID, "PLAY BALL!"*

"'Play Ball!' does a splendid job of making us think about how life imitates sport. Some is delightfully tongue-in-cheek, while most is carefully crafted to provide a context in which we can consider whether we are on God's team....The roster spot is open. All we have to do is sign up."

JOHN RAWLINGS, SPORTING NEWS

"'Play Ball!' pulls off a near-miracle—an entirely fresh perspective on baseball, accomplished with wit and insight. The parallels between baseball and the Bible are fascinating."

LARRY STONE, THE SEATTLE TIMES

"With wit, some great baseball stories and a good head for analysis, Graf helps readers ponder the mysteries of life and baseball....It's all in good fun, but with a passion to help people find inspiration both on the playing field and in the Bible."

ST. LOUIS POST-DISPATCH

"A rollicking and inspiring tribute...Graf's skillful interweaving of sport and Scripture never trivializes faith, but rather makes its mysteries easier to grasp."

UNITED METHODIST REVIEW

"Graf has cleverly blended major league baseball and the Bible into a very entertaining and highly informative book, which will lead even the casual reader to a greater appreciation of the world of both sport and Spirit."

NORMAN J. MUCKERMAN, C.SS.R.,

FORMER PRESIDENT, CATHOLIC PRESS ASSOCIATION

Other Books by Gary Graf
available from Liguori Publications

And God Said, "It's Good!"
Amusing and Thought-Provoking Parallels
Between the Bible and Football

And God Said, "Tee it Up!"
Amusing and Thought-Provoking Parallels
Between the Bible and Golf

And God Said, "PLAY BALL!"

Amusing and Thought-Provoking Parallels Between the Bible and Baseball

Gary Graf

Photographs by Jack Zehrt

Liguori

Imprimi Potest:
Thomas D. Picton, C.Ss.R.
Provincial, Denver Province
The Redemptorists

Published by Liguori/Triumph
An imprint of Liguori Publications
Liguori, Missouri
www.liguori.org

Library of Congress Cataloging-in-Publication Data

Graf, Gary.
    And God said, "Play ball!": amusing and thought-provoking parallels between the Bible and baseball / Gary Graf.
        p.   cm.
    Includes bibliographical references.
    ISBN 978-0-7648-1475-4 (pbk)
    1. Bible—Criticism, interpretation, etc.—Miscellanea. 2. Baseball—Religious aspects—Christianity. 3. Baseball—History—Miscellanea. I. Title.

BS538.G63   2005
220—dc22   2004061576

The editor and publisher gratefully acknowledge permission to reprint/reproduce copyrighted works granted by the publishers/sources listed on pages 179–180.

Printed in the United States of America
17 16 15 14 13 / 11 10 9 8 7

Contents

CONTENTS

Foreword

GOD MUST SMILE SOMEWHAT WHIMSICALLY when he looks at us baseball fans. He might even think, "What *have* I wrought?" We are loud, bordering on obnoxious; we are absolutely blind to the facts about our own team, and the man in charge is always wrong when calls go against our team. For some, baseball has even replaced religion as the focus of life. All very unchristian attributes, wouldn't you say?

I think he must smile compassionately, though, when he considers us in other ways.

At least some of the language and many of the ideals are similar in baseball and Christianity. After all, we frequently refer to the place where the game is played as a cathedral. We all admire a skilled player who is willing and able to make a sacrifice for the team. We engage in fierce debate about the origin of the game of baseball, and we find some differences in the Creation stories in the Bible. God must appreciate the passion that goes into playing the game well—at whatever level—just as he admires the passion we pour into pursuing his will for us. Baseball has its rulebook; God handed down his rule book...and both are open for interpretation in many places. OK, I'll acknowledge one substantial difference: In baseball, a hitter who fails 67 percent of the time is considered Hall of Fame material. I'm pretty sure God has a higher standard for us in his field of play.

Baseball, perhaps more than any other sport, relies on teammates understanding their roles and carrying out assigned duties to achieve success. Isn't God's kingdom built on exactly the same foundation? Those who can preach should preach. Those who can teach should teach. It's up to each of us to understand what God's plan is and build our lives around that.

When I think about God and baseball, I am always brought back to one unique man I am fortunate to call a friend, Johnny Oates. Johnny was a major league catcher for eleven years and a two-time Manager of the Year for the Baltimore Orioles and Texas Rangers. More than four years ago, Johnny was stricken with an extremely invasive form of brain cancer. When we talked the first time after the diagnosis, I was more tearful than he was. "I can't wait to see what God has in store for me," Johnny said and the words ring in my ears every day.

Gary Graf does a splendid job of making us think about how life imitates sport in *And God Said, "Play Ball!"* Some is delightfully tongue-in-cheek, while most is carefully crafted to provide a context in which we can consider whether we are on God's team. The offer is there from God, the roster spot open. All we have to do is sign up.

JOHN RAWLINGS
SENIOR VICE PRESIDENT/EDITORIAL DIRECTOR
THE SPORTING NEWS

Acknowledgments

AS WITH MOST SUCCESSFUL TEAMS on the baseball field, this book is the culmination of the efforts, talents, and sacrifices of a sterling lineup. At the top of the order are Paul Pennick and Joseph Nonnenkamp of Liguori Publications. Without their combined interest and guidance, encouragement and expertise, the book you hold in your hands would not have come into being.

On a personal level, I would like to thank Fathers Craig Boley, Bob Camuso, and Chris Weekly for breaking open the word of God for me and thousands of others in the Seattle area. Thanks to St. Joseph Parish in Seattle for inviting me to learn of the value of community through service. A special thanks to Pam Goodfellow for her encouragement and words of writing wisdom, and to Vanessa Gallant for her unflagging support and infectious pride in my work.

In closing, I would like to especially thank my sister, Jacki, for joining me on tours of major league baseball stadiums around the country—fourteen and counting. A most heartfelt thank you to my parents, Kenneth and Dorothy, and kids, Betsy and Brian, the bookends of my life. And a humble thank you to God for saying, "Play Ball!" in the first place!

Liguori Publications and the author would like to express our deepest gratitude to Jack Zehrt for his contributions to *And God Said, "Play Ball!"* Mr. Zehrt's classic baseball photographs add a richness to this book that would otherwise be missing in their absence. His enthusiasm and assistance in choosing images for this book were invaluable to the editors.

And God Said, "PLAY BALL!"

"I BELIEVE IN THE CHURCH OF BASEBALL."

Annie Savoy, Bull Durham[1]

"I believe that you are the Messiah."

JOHN 11:27

AS A YOUNGSTER, I GREW UP MEMORIZING the teachings of the *Baltimore Catechism* and the lineup of the San Francisco Giants. Evenings ended with prayers, mornings began with box scores. I studied both the verses of the Bible and statistics of baseball... religiously. I collected holy cards featuring saints and prayers, and baseball cards touting stats and players. The former came with grace; the latter with bubble gum, a flat, pink rectangle of chewable sweetness. Nothing seemed more divine.

My uniform of the day alternated between the designated parochial school attire of salt-and-pepper corduroys, white short-sleeve shirt, and forest green button-up sweater and the scratchy, almost indestructible flannel pants and team jerseys of Stanaway Brothers Grocery, Les Moresco Builders, and—perhaps as a reminder that we are but a moment's notice from that great dugout in the sky—Chapel of the Highlands Mortuary. I learned of the miracle of the loaves and fishes and the Miracle of Coogan's Bluff. And I must confess that pennant races between the Giants and Dodgers inspired more prayers than most Sunday sermons.

St. Dunstan Church outside of San Francisco and Seals Stadium within the city were my respective places of worship. My childhood church was quite modest in comparison to St. Patrick's Cathedral in New York. But to the fifty students in my second grade class, its peaked roof seem to rise to the heavens themselves. The sturdy wood rafters that held the roof above us lent an air of solidity and strength. Endless rows of honey-stained pews greeted us on entry, and a larger-than-life Jesus nailed to the cross above the altar beseeched us to be good boys and girls.

Priests in colorful and elaborate vestments celebrated the Mass in Latin. Certain gestures occasioned bells to be rung by altar boys. Beeswax candles burned bright, giving off an ethereal glow. The sweet aroma of incense filled the air. A choir sung celestial hymns accompanied by music from an unseen organ. Each element of the Mass added more to the mystique of my religion. I remember one Mass in particular. There, hanging over the altar, the forlorn figure of Jesus, his blood-caked hands and feet nailed to the cross, a gaping wound in his side. His pleading eyes held me in their gaze. I could not turn away. Minutes—it seemed like hours—passed before I was released. Such could be the pull of my faith.

San Francisco's Seals Stadium was a pale comparison to its New York cousin, Yankee Stadium, or even the old Polo Grounds. Seals was a minor league park literally and figuratively, a single level, cigar-box venue, holding only 22,900 fans, less than half of the capacity of today's modern ball yards. But to a nine-year-old boy celebrating his birthday with his parents, it had all the grandeur of a cathedral. My first walk through the tunnel leading to my seat between first base and the right field foul pole took my breath away. It was a wondrous sight of lush green, illuminated by banks of bright lights. The infield dirt looked as if it were groomed with a comb, the bases were sparkling soft pillows of white, the four corners of a perfect diamond. I had never seen so many rows of seats before.

Vendors wrestled with containers, holding every kind of delectable treat—but especially the hot dog with brown, spicy mustard. (They never tasted like this at home.) Peanut and popcorn smells filled the air. The cream-colored uniforms of the home team Giants gleamed in angelic hues, while the road grays of the Phillies gave off a hint of dirt and deviltry.

On the field, third-base coaches offered a mime of flashing hand and arm motions, sending silent, secret signals that only batters and baserunners could decipher. Thousands roared in appreciation or derision of close calls by the umpires. Organ music rallied the clapping fans at crucial moments during the game. It was an exhilarating experience, a thrill of my short lifetime. It left me wanting more.

So while the gospels of Matthew and Mark were giving nourishment to my soul, the feats of Mays and McCovey were taking hold of my heart. It was not easy to know which held more meaning for me as a youth: my first Communion or my first major league baseball game. Both were spiritual experiences.

Communion made me eligible to receive the major league sacrament of the Catholic Church, ingesting the bread transformed into the body of Christ just as Jesus ordained during the Last Supper on the night before his death. Of course as a second-grader at the time, all this was beyond me. I likened the host, an unleavened thin disc of bread, to a white Necco Wafer, a popular candy of the day. The host, as you might expect, was not nearly as tasty.

At that first game at Seals Stadium, I was overjoyed to be in the presence of my heroes whose exploits I had read about, dreamed of, listened to, committed to memory. Yet, on that September night in 1959, I was unaware of the ballet performed around second base with the turning of a double play, nor the deception practiced by a pitcher throwing a changeup. I had no clue that three future Hall of Famers performed for me that evening: pitcher Robin Roberts, the hard-throwing Philadelphia Phillie right-hander; center fielder Willie Mays, said by many to be one of the greatest ever to play the game;

and Willie McCovey, a tall, lanky rookie first baseman who would become one of the most feared sluggers in baseball.

Communion and baseball, I was just happy to be there. I had no deep understanding of either. Since then I have grown to appreciate their intricacies, subtleties, profundities, and, even their commonalities. In the intervening years, I have struggled with my faith and at times the direction of baseball. Yet, both continue to have a hold on me, tugging at something deep inside. I keep returning. Each has taught me lessons about love, loss, and life. Each has its own rewards, its version of universal truth. Each reveals a wondrous glimpse into what it is to be human. I'm no theologian, and I was never very good with a curve ball, but I marvel at the symbiosis, the intimate connection between that which is heaven sent…and the game which is heaven on earth.

This book is a joint expression of two of my greatest loves: baseball and the Bible. It is, however, in no way meant to be an exegesis (interpretation) of the Bible. I am not a biblical scholar and don't pretend to be one here. Some of my observations on the Bible and its connections to baseball are just that…observations. They are at times, I hope, thought-provoking, challenging, curious, and—sometimes—amusing. Perhaps through this book readers will learn to love the Good Book and great game as I do. And realize that there is a great deal to be learned about life through both.

It's said that God is present everywhere. For me this is nowhere more true than on a baseball field. In fact, I expect that baseball may just well be the secular version of God's grace to us all. So step up to the plate and make the sign of the cross. There's a lot we can learn from angels, both guardian and those from Anaheim.

"PLAY BALL!"

Home plate umpire at the start of every baseball game.

And God saw that it was good.

GENESIS 1:10

SINCE THE BEGINNING OF TIME, people have had a preoccupation with, well, the beginning of time. Every culture has its own creation myth, the biblical stories of Genesis included. Scientists try to pinpoint, within a few billion years, the big bang that started it all. To get a sense of our own history, we ask our parents, "Mommy, how did you and Daddy meet?"

As human beings we struggle with fundamental questions: Who are we? Why are we here? How do you throw a curve ball?

We search for our place in the universe. If we can't say with any certainty where we are ultimately headed, then we do our best to determine from whence we came. Creation tales provide us with a starting point and, if we're lucky, our marching orders. They become the touchstones that connect us to our planet, to one another.

The same can be said about faith and baseball.

Because of our desire for origins, stories with wonderful beginnings tend to captivate and hold us. Two of the best can be found in the creation of the game of baseball, not to mention of life itself. Take a look at the respective Bibles of American baseball and Christian faith, *Baseball: An Illustrated History* by Geoffrey C. Ward and documentary filmmaker Ken Burns, and the real thing, *The Holy Bible*, in this case the *New Revised Standard Version*.

Ask any baseball player or fan worth his weight in Bobble Head Dolls about the origins of the game, and you are likely to hear the name of the game's inventor, Abner Doubleday. Messrs. Ward and Burns recount that

> One summer afternoon in 1839, at Cooperstown, on the shore of Otsego Lake in upstate New York, the boys of the Otsego Academy were playing a game of town ball against Green's Select School. The rules of town ball were so loose that every hit was fair, and the boys sometimes ran headlong into one another. That day, a resourceful young Otsego player named Abner Doubleday sat down and, on the spot, drew up the rules for a brand-new game, and called it baseball. Doubleday would eventually become a hero at the Battle of Gettysburg, and his game would become the national pastime.[1]

Other memorable starts come to mind: William Boeing visits an air show and declares, "I think we can build a better airplane." After losing the rights to his cartoon character Oswald the Rabbit, Walt Disney creates Mickey Mouse on a train ride from New York to Hollywood. Even the sport of basketball can trace its origins to a bit of Americana. James Naismith had his young charges heave a round ball into peach baskets at a Springfield, Massachusetts, YMCA. In the modern era, "The Steves," Sculley and Jobs, invent Apple Computer in their garage. Bill Gates drops out of Harvard to form Microsoft with Paul Allen.

So it should come as no surprise that baseball sprang from the mind of young Doubleday in bucolic upstate New York. That's why the baseball Hall of Fame resides in Cooperstown after all. That's why the ballpark there is called Doubleday Field.

You don't have to look too far to see Abner's fingerprints on his grand plan either—a hit in which a batter safely reaches second base is called a "double." It's not too difficult to envision how playing two of Doubleday's games in a single sunlit afternoon came to be called a "double header."

However, Ward and Burns add, "...or so the old story had it."[2]

Apparently, while he was a distinguished Civil War hero, firing one of the first federal guns from Fort Sumter in 1861, Abner Doubleday was at West Point, not Cooperstown, during that fine summer in question. As Ward and Burns put it, "He never claimed to have had anything to do with baseball, and may never have even seen a game."[3]

Baseball shades of Sidd Finch, the fictional New York Mets pitching phenom that *Sports Illustrated*, via the gifted pen of George Plimpton, foisted on its readers one April Fools' Day in 1985.

As our nation's early spin doctors presented our first president, George Washington, as larger than life, so too has baseball undergone a cultural makeover. With George, we were taught that he chopped down the cherry tree, never told a lie, and hurled a silver dollar across the Potomac River. Our only question was whether he used a two- or four-seam fastball grip on the coin. That Washington, as well as Jefferson and many of our founding fathers, owned slaves didn't seem to make the media guide of those times.

Through no fault of his own, Abner Doubleday became Abner doublecross. In *Baseball: More Than 150 Years*, authors David Nemec and Saul Wizen elaborate:

> At that time public debate raged over whether baseball was purely an American creation, the view argued by Albert Spalding [he of the sporting goods company of the same name], or whether it was a descendant of British games such as rounders.... As a pubic relations maneuver, Spalding arranged for a rigged blue-ribbon commission [The Mills Commission of 1907] to name Doubleday as the father of baseball....In the words of Harold Peterson, "Abner Doubleday didn't invent baseball; baseball invented Abner Doubleday."[4]

In terms of veracity, it appears baseball stumbled right out of the batter's box. But trickery is part of the game of life. For instance, the first book of the Bible, Genesis, reveals that Jacob obtained his father's blessing under duplicitous circumstances. Tradition held that older brother, Esau, was in line for the family birthright, which in this case just happened to be the ancestral covenant that Abraham, Jacob's grandfather, made with God. Could baseball's first fans have been similarly fooled?

If the Doubleday story was scored an error, how then did base-ball come about? Let's see what happens in the game's next at bat.

It turns out that our national pastime was actually inspired by many nations. After all, our country has no underlying nationality, but instead came to be by virtue of a mix of peoples seeking religious freedom. These first settlers brought with them their books of worship and their own favorite games of play. Two of the most prominent from which baseball derives many similarities come from England—cricket and rounders. These games inspired colonial counterparts with such names as barn ball, stickball, round ball, base, and even base ball (two words).

Burns and Ward describe an early game of baseball: a square infield, no fixed positions, up to fifty players scattered about. A feeder tossed the ball to the striker who was allowed to demand that the ball arrive either high or low, and then wait and wait if necessary, until he got his wish. One out retired the side, and a runner was out if the ball was caught on the fly or he was "soaked," or hit, with the ball while running the bases.[5] Fortunately, the game underwent a refinement or two.

What has become the game we play today had its true begin-nings in New York City during the "Summer of '42"—1842, that is.

Sometime during the spring or summer of 1842, a group of young gentlemen began getting together in Manhattan each weekend to play one or another version of the game, depending upon how many showed up at game time. They played first on a vacant lot at the corner of Madison Avenue and Twenty-Seventh Street, then in a slightly more spacious clearing at the foot of Murray Hill.[6]

Obviously, refinements would have to be made. After all, if they put first base at Madison and Twenty-Seventh and put second base at Murray Hill, that's an awful long way to leg out a double! But it's like batting against the Chicago Cubs' pitcher Greg Maddux. You know a change is going to come, you just don't know when.

In this case that change came three years later on September 23, 1845. On that date, twenty-eight of the fine fellows in the group mentioned above, apparently at the urging of a twenty-five-year-old shipping clerk named Alexander Joy Cartwright, Jr., created the game's first baseball team—the New York Knickerbocker Base Ball Club.

The Knickerbockers decreed that the infield be diamond-shaped, rather than square. First and third bases were set at forty-two paces apart. The balk was identified and outlawed. Foul lines were established. Pitchers were to throw the ball underhanded, keeping the elbow and wrist straight. The batter got three missed swings before he was called out. Most important, runners were to be tagged or thrown out, not thrown *at*.[7]

If all this is true, how could we be under the spell of the Double-day myth for so long? Actually, it's not too hard to imagine. One explanation might be that we were desperate for our own identity, our own heroes, our own stories and history. So early editions of the America PR machine gave us folklore, far and wide. Rather than focus on George's wooden teeth, we have Washington and his silver dollar, and his never-tell-a-lie persona. To explain the foul smell of buckskins in our nation's capitol, we hear of frontier-taming, bear-wrasslin'

Davy Crockett. In our youthful exuberance, and perhaps to impress more established cultures, our stories took on more mythical proportions. Thus, we had John (Johnny Appleseed) Chapman walking the land planting apple trees, and war hero, baseball-inventing Abner Doubleday himself.

Who really knows how legends develop? Our ancestors, in search of religious freedom, brought with them one of the greatest sources of storytelling ever compiled: the Bible. Steeped in the Good Book's penchant for storytelling and maybe a looser interpretation of historical accuracy, baseball lore may have been embellished along the lines of the Holy Bible.

In the Bible, life is so wondrous a concept that the world was created twice. Or at least it was recorded as such in the first chapter of Genesis.

SCENE 1, TAKE 1

In the beginning when God created the heavens and the earth, the earth was a formless void and darkness covered the face of the deep, while a wind from God swept over the face of the waters. Then God said, "Let there be light"; and there was light. And God saw that the light was good; and God separated the light from the darkness. God called the light Day, and the darkness he called Night. And there was evening and there was morning, the first day (Genesis 1:1–5).

In similar fashion, for the next five days God kept adding to his creation. On the second day came the oceans and sky. The third day brought about dry land and with it grass, herbs, and fruit trees. On the fourth day, God created the sun and the moon. By the end of the fifth day, our Creator had given the command: "Be fruitful and multiply" to the creatures of the sea, the birds of the air and all the animals that roamed the land. On the sixth day, God said,

"Let us make humankind in our image, according to our likeness; and let them have dominion over the fish of the sea, and over the birds of the air, and over the cattle, and over all the wild animals of the earth, and over every creeping thing that creeps upon the earth."
So God created humankind in his image,
in the image of God he created them;
male and female he created them.
God blessed them, and God said to them, "Be fruitful and multiply, and fill the earth and subdue it; and have dominion over the fish of the sea and over the birds of the air and over every living thing that moves upon the earth...." God saw everything that he had made, and indeed, it was very good (Genesis 1:26–28, 31).

Not content with one creation story, the authors of the Book of Genesis included a second, adopting a similar philosophy summarized thousands of years later so succinctly by Chicago Cub great Ernie Banks, "Great day for baseball! Let's play two!"

Which brings us to Genesis 2:4–7, 18–23. Or Creation, the Sequel.

SCENE 1, TAKE 2

These are the generations of the heavens and the earth when they were created. In the day that the LORD *God made the earth and the heavens, when no plant of the field was yet in the earth and... there was no one to till the ground; but a stream would rise from the earth, and water the whole face of the ground—then the* LORD *God formed man from the dust of the ground, and breathed into his nostrils the breath of life; and the man became a living being.*

Then the LORD *God said, "It is not good that the man should be alone; I will make him a helper as his partner." So out of the ground the* LORD *God formed every animal of the field and every bird of the air, and brought them to the man to see what he would*

ı; *and whatever the man called every living creature, that was*
. *The man gave names to all cattle, and to the birds of the air,*
and to every animal of the field; but for the man there was not found
a helper as his partner. So the LORD *God caused a deep sleep to fall*
upon the man, and he slept; then he took one of his ribs and closed
up its place with flesh. And the rib that the LORD *God had taken*
from the man he made into a woman and brought her to the man.
Then the man said,
"This at last is bone of my bones
and flesh of my flesh;
this one shall be called Woman,
for out of Man this one was taken."

As one can see, there are a few discrepancies in these accounts.
Did God create the heavens and then the earth (Take 1)? Or the
earth and then the heavens (Take 2)? Did God create the birds of
the sky, the beasts of the earth, and then man and woman (Take
1)? Or did he create Adam first, the creatures second, and Eve third
(Take 2)? And finally, did Babe Ruth actually call his shot against
pitcher Charlie Root in the 1932 World Series against the Cubs or
not? Inquiring minds want to know.

In the 1996 book *Genesis: A Living Conversation*, from the PBS
television series of the same name, host Bill Moyers brought together
thirty-eight commentators to discuss, as the title suggests, Genesis.
Among Moyers' colleagues were Catholics, Protestants, Jews, Mus-
lims, Hindus, priests, rabbis, men, women, parents, divorcees, artists,
authors, professors, a psychotherapist, a journalist, a lawyer—in
short, nearly everyone except a baseball player. In a series of fascinating conversations—often contentious, usually provocative, always
illuminating—some of the most well-known stories from Genesis
were discussed, including the two creation tales.

Several issues were raised. Is the first creation story just the big
picture, whereas the second provides us with more detail? Or are

they separate accounts? Does the second creation story suggest that Eve is subordinate to Adam, and thus women to men, because she was created from Adam's rib? Or do women share the higher place through Eve's being created last, an argument supported by other biblical stories where the last born was the preferred or most important: Isaac over Ishmael, Jacob over Esau, Joseph over his brothers. Or are men and women equal in God's eyes because he created them simultaneously in Creation One? Perhaps God seemed too aloof and removed from we humans in the first tale. So a second story was created that brought God in direct contact with mankind and made it easier for us to believe that we humans are truly of God.

One of the commentators, Rabbi Burton Visotsky, throws us another curve:

> It's even a little more complicated than that. In one story, humanity is created in one fell swoop, which implies man and woman are equal. And it also suggests something about how we read God—that God can't simply be seen as he. If humanity reflects God, we have to understand that God has both male and female aspects in some miraculous way.[8]

Sorting it all out is nearly as difficult as explaining the infield fly rule to a baseball newcomer. Could the answer be as simple as two sportswriters covering the same game from different points of view? Certainly the *Boston Globe* had a different take on the Red Sox victory over the Yankees in the 2004 playoffs than did the *New York Post*.

Quite possibly each creation account became part of the oral tradition of different audiences of ages past as elders and storytellers gave reason to the fundamental questions that people have grappled with since the beginning of time—how did we get here?

This query has taken on new meaning with modern discoveries of the universe made possible by the Hubble telescope and other advances of science. *New York Times* author Kenneth C. Davis in his book *Don't Know Much About the Bible* summarized the issue quite nicely:

> Here is the great raging war of the last few centuries reduced to a nutshell. How do you balance a belief that the world was created by divine pronouncement, a mere 6,000 years ago, with the scientific observation that modern humans walked 117,000 years ago and a galaxy was born 13 billion years ago? This is the war between science and faith.[9]

And you thought DiMaggio versus Williams sparked debate!

So, fact or fiction? How did mankind, and baseball, come to be? We have two accounts of each. What truly happened? On the one hand, our ever-questioning nature wants the certainty that comes with knowing definitively. But does it really matter?

Creation is such an incomprehensible concept that cultures have long tried to grasp it by putting form to a story that we can relate to on a more human level. We do this not to diminish the glory or wonder of creation, but to praise it, to honor it in a way that we can pass down from generation to generation. What's significant is that in its logical, illogical, and mythological form, the Bible can teach us, guide us, and inspire us to grow closer to God and one another.

As for baseball, it's such a grand affair that people wish, almost demand, that its origins match the loftiness and mythic proportion the game has attained in our national consciousness. If Abner Doubleday didn't invent baseball, well, as a West Pointer, as a Civil War hero, as an American, he darn well *could* have.

Yes, we care about the true origins of our selves and our game. But is our love for baseball any less because Doubleday didn't invent it? Does our awe of the cosmos diminish because it was created in a split second and not six days, or vice versa? Our overwhelming sense of joy and gratitude comes when we marvel that both creation and baseball have been allowed to *be* in the first place.

"PAIR UP IN THREES."1

Yogi Berra

*He called the twelve and began to
send them out two by two.*

MARK 6:7

TWENTY-EIGHT GENTLEMEN formed the first bona fide baseball
team in 1845. Brought together by Alexander Cartwright, Jr., the
roster counted among its members merchants, insurance salesmen,
investment brokers, a U.S. marshal, a portrait photographer, a doctor, a cigar dealer—in short, prosperous men who were available for
a game most days by mid-afternoon. Kind of like Cub fans today.

From that first team the game grew to neighborhood contests
and borough battles in and around New York. A *New York Mercury*
sportswriter referred to the game as "the National Pastime"2 in the
winter of 1856, even though the game had not yet ventured very far
beyond the East or Hudson rivers. But then, for many New Yorkers
then (and even today) that is the extent of the civilized world.

Similarly, the early followers of Christ referred to his teachings as The Way despite being concentrated, even with Saint Paul's
evangelizing journeys, to small pockets of the Middle East and the
Mediterranean.

As for the growth of baseball, it wasn't long before the game
was being played on farms, in towns, in colleges, by Union soldiers
under Confederate guard and, in 1890, even a barnstorming ladies
team in bloomers.

In 1869 the first truly professional baseball team, the Cincinnati Red Stockings, took the field, backed by a group of Ohio investors. These days all we hear about is the dire financial straits of small-market franchises, and the possibility of contraction—closing down some major league teams in cities where they receive meager support. These small-market teams that are losing money could take a lesson from their professional forebears, the Red Stockings. That club was profitable in its very first season, posting a robust $1.39 on the black side of the ledger.[3] Of course, the next year when the red hose lost to the best team in the east, the Brooklyn Atlantics, fan support evaporated and the team folded. As the first professional baseball team, the Red Stockings also became the first professional baseball team to move to a different city.

In 1871, the now *Boston* Red Stockings became one of the charter teams of the new National Association of Professional Base Ball Players, along with the Chicago White Stockings, Cleveland Forest Citys, Fort Wayne Kekiongas, New York Mutuals, Philadelphia Athletics, Rockford Forest Citys, Troy Haymakers, and Washington Olympics.

In 1876, owners' egos and the lure of the dollar for players caused the game to change. That year the best player of his era, Cap Anson, jumped from the Philadelphia Athletics to the Chicago White Stockings, helping to usher in the new and improved National League of Professional Base Ball Clubs, with Boston, Chicago, Cincinnati, Hartford, Louisville, Philadelphia, New York, and St. Louis as charter members. Not surprisingly, these large cities of the day became the first big market clubs of baseball.

The early churches of Christianity also emerged in the large cities or towns perched along trade routes or near ports, even though entire congregations may have numbered only thirty believers. A look at Paul's epistles provides a glimpse of some of these nascent Christian centers: Rome; Corinth; the region of Galatia including Antioch, Iconium, Lystra, Derbe, and Tarsus; Ephesus, the capital of the Roman province of Asia, today a part of Turkey; Philippi in what is now present-day Greece; Colosse, about a hundred-mile road trip east of Ephesus; and Thessalonica, located on the northwest corner of the Aegean Sea, considered on the continent of Europe. With his epistles, Paul was the equivalent of today's itinerant writers for *Sports Illustrated*, traveling to all the major league cities covering the top teams, doling out advice, offering criticism, scolding when needed, praising in proportion.

Back to the game of baseball.

For the next quarter century the National League held sway as rival leagues came and went. It wasn't until 1900 when the new American League was established—with teams in Buffalo, Chicago, Cleveland, Detroit, Kansas City, Indianapolis, Milwaukee, and Minneapolis—that the National League had a worthy adversary. Intra-league squabbles such as they were in those days were put aside when the first "World Series" was played in 1903, with the Boston Pilgrims beating the Pittsburgh Pirates, five games to three.

A number of our present-day franchises can trace their roots to these formative years, with "genealogies" of seemingly biblical proportions. For instance, the Boston Red Stockings begot the Boston Braves who begot the Milwaukee Braves who begot the Atlanta team of the same name. Remarkably, the Braves have played every year since the National League was founded in 1871, the only franchise to do so.

New York's legendary Yankees club actually began play in that city in 1903 as the Highlanders, after relocating from Baltimore where they were the Orioles. Today's Baltimore Orioles were once the St. Louis Browns (as were the St. Louis Cardinals, back in 1881), having moved there from Milwaukee. The Cleveland Indians were at one time known as the Naps, the Broncos, and originally the Blues, after the color of their uniforms.

More begotting:

The Boston Americans begot the Pilgrims as well as the Puritans, Plymouth Rocks, and Somersets, all of whom eventually begot the

Red Sox. Before moving to San Francisco, the New York Giants were known as the Gothams. Speaking of moving, the Philadelphia Athletics became the Kansas City Athletics on their way to becoming the Oakland Athletics. And before the Dodgers came to wear Los Angeles on their uniforms, they called Brooklyn their home, where they were known as the Bridegrooms, Superbas, and, after settling in at Ebbets Field with its trolley tracks, the Trolley Dodgers, not to mention "da bums."

Even the Chicago Cubs began their colorful history as the Chicago White Stockings, a notion nearly blasphemous considering how rabid Cub and White Sox fans are for their teams today. Founded in 1870, the Cub club is the oldest franchise to have played in the same city. No wonder they're so loved! Had it not been for play being suspended for two years due to the Chicago fire, they would hold the record for the longest continuously running franchise.

As the game spread far and wide, players came from near and far. Pepper Martin of the St. Louis Cardinals' Gas House Gang was at one time a hobo. Teammate Dizzy Dean dropped out of school in second grade, later confessing, "I didn't do so well in the first grade either."[4] New York Yankee great Babe Ruth was an orphan from Baltimore, while Lou Gehrig was lured from Columbia University. Brooklyn Dodger star Jackie Robinson was a college football star and became the first African-American to break baseball's color barrier. Hall of Famers Hank Greenberg of the Detroit Tigers and Sandy Koufax of the Dodgers were both Jewish. The 1950 Philadelphia Phillies seemed so young they acquired the moniker "Whiz Kids" on their way to the National League Pennant. In 1959, Luis Aparicio (Venezuela) and Nellie Fox (Pennsylvania), neither of whom weighed more than 160 pounds, led the Go-Go (Chicago White) Sox to the American League pennant.

All this is to say that today's baseball teams are made up of as varied a group of human beings as you can throw together on a diamond. Different races, nationalities, faiths, educations, heights, weights, and shoe sizes. Yet all pulling together with one goal in mind. What the Knickerbockers started as a single base ball club for prosperous New Yorkers (all of whom were white mind you) has now matured into a game that is known, played, and loved around the world.

Sort of like Christianity.

My religion, my faith tradition—Catholicism—had its start in a very similar fashion to baseball with the formation of a team—in this case, the Galilee Apostles of the old River Jordan League.

At the risk of condensing a good part of the New Testament into a single sentence, Jesus, the Son of God, was born of Mary, preached, taught, was crucified, died and was buried, only to rise three days later, thereby conquering sin and death, and showing us the way home to God the Father. When the time came for Jesus to begin his ministry, the preaching of his father's word, he handpicked a group of men to accompany him. In other words, he selected his own team. Gospel writer Luke records the "draft" this way:

Once while Jesus was standing beside the lake of Gennesaret, and the crowd was pressing in on him to hear the word of God, he saw two boats there at the shore of the lake; the fishermen had gone out of them and were washing their nets. He got into one of the boats, the one belonging to Simon, and asked him to put out a little way from the shore. Then he sat down and taught the crowds from the boat. When he had finished speaking, he said to Simon, "Put out into the deep water and let down your nets for a catch." Simon answered, "Master, we have worked all night long but have caught nothing. Yet if you say so, I will let down the nets." When they had done this, they caught so many fish that their nets were beginning to break. So they signaled their partners in the other boat to come and help them. And they came and filled both boats, so that they began to sink. But when Simon Peter saw it, he fell down at Jesus' knees, saying, "Go away from me, Lord, for I am a sinful man!" For he and all who were with him were amazed at the catch of fish that they had taken; and so also were James and John, sons of Zebedee, who were partners with Simon. Then Jesus said to Simon, "Do not be afraid; from now on you will be catching people." When they had brought their boats to shore, they left everything and followed him (Luke 5:1–11).

I should point out that baseball's future is hinted at, dare I say predicted, in Luke. In perhaps a most startling foretelling of baseball deeds to come, *For he and all who were with him were amazed at the catch* must no doubt refer to the 52,571 fans who witnessed Willie Mays' incredible catch of Vic Wertz's smash in deep center field during the first game of the 1954 World Series between Mays' New York Giants and Wertz's Cleveland Indians.

Now let Matthew tell you in his own words how it was he came to be an apostle:

As Jesus was walking along, he saw a man called Matthew sitting at the tax booth; and he said to him, "Follow me." And he got up and followed him.

And as he sat at dinner in the house, many tax collectors and sinners came and were sitting with him and his disciples. When the Pharisees saw this, they said to his disciples, "Why does your teacher eat with tax collectors and sinners?" But when he heard this, he said, "Those who are well have no need of a physician, but those who are sick. Go and learn what this means, 'I desire mercy, not sacrifice.' For I have come to call not the righteous but sinners" (Matthew 9:9–13).

A little background: Pharisees were Jewish secular leaders of the day; it was their job to interpret and encourage the law of Moses, the Scriptures, and a whole body of oral traditions. Tax collectors were usually Jews working for the Roman government. Any money over and above what was owed Rome would inevitably line their pockets. Needless to say, they were not well liked among their brethren as their wealth came at the people's expense. Thus when most everyone else Matthew came in contact with wanted very little to do with him, Jesus chose this tax collector to be included in his inner circle. No wonder Matthew was overjoyed to "play" for this team. He must have felt the same sort of elation that the skinny kid with glasses feels when he's picked to play on a team when the bigger, better neighborhood boys choose sides for a game.

In John's Gospel, we learn of the drafting of more "players."

The next day Jesus decided to go to Galilee. He found Philip and said to him, "Follow me." Now Philip was from Bethsaida, the city of Andrew and Peter. Philip found Nathanael and said to him, "We have found him about whom Moses in the law and also the prophets wrote, Jesus son of Joseph from Nazareth." Nathaneal said to him, "Can anything good come out of Nazareth?" Philip said to him, "Come and see." When Jesus saw Nathanael coming toward him, he said..."I saw you under the fig tree before Philip called you." Nathanael replied, "Rabbi, you are the Son of God! You are the King of Israel!" (John 1:43–49).

A little background, part two. Though Nazareth is well known today as the place where Jesus was raised, during the period he called it home, it was a tiny village of no importance. Thus Nathanael's statement, *"Can anything good come out of Nazareth?"* Jesus' hometown was so small, so insignificant that one truly had to wonder if anything worthwhile could come from such a place, especially someone important, someone of whom Moses wrote in the Scriptures.

One can imagine such thoughts going through managers' and teammates' minds when newcomers arrive on the big league scene. Can this son of a coal miner be any good? Can this boy fresh out of high school really play ball? Can a guy who committed 58 errors in the minors make it in The Show? Well, for Hall of Famers Mickey Mantle, Al Kaline, and Rogers Hornsby, respectively, the answer was obviously, "Darn straight!"

As for the rest of the draft, Mark summarizes it this way:

He went up the mountain and called to him those whom he wanted, and they came to him. And he appointed twelve, whom he also named apostles, to be with him, and to be sent out to proclaim the message, and to have authority to cast out demons. So he appointed the twelve: Simon (to whom he gave the name Peter); James son of Zebedee and John the brother of James (to whom he gave the name Boanerges, that is, Sons of Thunder); and Andrew, and Philip, and Bartholomew, and Matthew, and Thomas, and James son of Alphaeus, and Thaddaeus, and Simon the Cananaean, and Judas Iscariot, who betrayed him. Then he went home (Mark 3:13–19).

Think about this for a second. The group of men that Jesus assembled to bring God's word to the world consisted of four fishermen, a tax collector, possibly a farmer or two, maybe a baker. Jesus himself was a carpenter. If after pondering the unlikeliness of it all, you still have trouble believing, then think about this for a moment. Members of the first organized baseball team, the Knickerbockers, included a photographer, an insurance salesman, and a cigar dealer.

"RUNS, HITS, ERRORS"

*Categories tallied at the end of
every inning of a baseball game*

Who can detect their errors?

PSALM 19:12

ASSEMBLING A TEAM doesn't guarantee success on the field. Take the 1962 Mets…please! As one of two expansion teams entering the league that year, the Mets were formed for the most part with players selected from other teams. Existing teams were allowed to protect so many players on their rosters with the expansion teams then picking from the remainder. Since the established ball clubs protected their brightest stars and most promising players, the Mets had little to choose from. And it showed. They lost 120 games that year, a twentieth-century record. What's amazing is that they won 40. They finished at the bottom of the league in batting, fielding, and pitching. And caused their colorful manager Casey Stengel to wonder in disbelief, "Can't anybody here play this game?[1]

For all their mishaps, the '62 Mets were not the worst team in baseball history. That dubious distinction went to the Cleveland Spiders, 1899 edition. Just before the start of that inglorious season, the Spiders' owners purchased the St. Louis Browns, calling them the Perfectos, and sent the best Cleveland players to Missouri. The remaining Spiders had no bite. They lost 134 games with only 34 victories. Fans boycotted their games and the team came to be known as the "Exiles," "Forsakens," and "Wanderers." They were so reviled at home, that they stayed on the road for 114 games. What's more, interest in the team was so low that there seems to be no record of a team photo being taken anytime during the year.2

Was it really any different when Jesus selected his team? Despite being the fortunate few who spent more time with Jesus than anyone, listening to him preach, walking with him, talking with him, staying with him, praying with him, being made aware of his inner- most thoughts, hopes, and fears, despite all this, they were still just learning the "game." In fact, there were times when they just didn't get it. Take, for instance, the Parable of the Sower.

"Listen! A sower went out to sow. And as he sowed, some seed fell on the path, and the birds came and ate it up. Other seed fell on rocky ground, where it did not have much soil, and it sprang up quickly, since it had no depth of soil. And when the sun rose, it was scorched; and since it had no root, it withered away. Other seed fell among thorns, and the thorns grew up and choked it, and it yielded no grain. Other seed fell into good soil and brought forth grain, growing up and increasing and yielding thirty and sixty and a hundredfold...."

When he was alone, those who were around him along with the twelve asked him about the parables....

And he said to them, "Do you not understand this parable? Then how will you understand all the parables? The sower sows the word. These are the ones on the path where the word is sown: when they hear, Satan immediately comes and takes away the word that is sown in them. And these are the ones sown on rocky ground: when they hear the word, they immediately receive it with joy. But they have no root, and endure only for a while; then, when trouble or persecution arises on account of the word, immediately they fall away. And others are those sown among the thorns: these are the ones who hear the word, but the cares of the world, and the lure of wealth, and the desire for other things come in and choke the word, and it yields nothing. And these are the ones sown on the good soil:

they hear the word and accept it and bear fruit, thirty and sixty and a hundredfold" (Mark 4:2–8, 10, 13–20).

Thank God, and Jesus, that the apostles did ask the meaning of the parables so that we all might receive the Word of God, and be among those who have ears so that we can hear and understand.

Just as Christ used parables to impart wisdom to his followers, baseball too has inspired its fair share of stories with lessons about life. Ernest Lawrence Thayer's famous poem *Casey at the Bat* teaches us that it's not enough to talk the talk, you've got to walk the walk. On the silver screen, *City Slickers* portrays how baseball serves as a thread binding father to son. *Bull Durham* shows us the value of passing our knowledge on to others. *Field of Dreams* reveals a tale of a son wanting to bond with his father, to reunite, to reconcile. *The Natural* tells a story of redemption, death, and resurrection.

Those chosen for extraordinary greatness often begin humbly. Hall of Famer Willie Mays was hitless in his first twelve times at the plate before he claimed his first major league safety. It was another thirteen at bats before he got his second. In two of his first three years, Pirate great Roberto Clemente hit just a few points better than .250. In his first season with Milwaukee, eventual major league home run king Hank Aaron mustered a modest thirteen round-trippers. All time strikeout leader and 324-game winner Nolan Ryan had a won-lost record of only 29–38 in his first five seasons.

So it should come as no surprise that Peter, the rock upon whom Christ built his church, the fledgling Christian community's leader from whom all popes trace their lineage, would have his moments of doubt in faith. For his part, Peter recognized Jesus' power and divinity. This fisherman who so loved the Lord often sought to imitate him. Ah, but while the flesh is willing, the spirit is sometimes weak.

Immediately he made the disciples get into the boat and go on ahead to the other side....When evening came...the boat, battered by the waves, was far from the land, for the wind was against them. And early in the morning he came walking toward them on the sea. But when the disciples saw him walking on the sea, they were terrified, saying, "It is a ghost!" And they cried out in fear. But immediately Jesus spoke to them and said, "Take heart, it is I; do not be afraid."

Peter answered him, "Lord, if it is you, command me to come to you on the water." He said, "Come." So Peter got out of the boat, started walking on the water, and came toward Jesus. But when he noticed the strong wind, he became frightened, and beginning to sink, he cried out, "Lord, save me!" Jesus immediately reached out his hand and caught him, saying to him, "You of little faith, why did you doubt?" (Matthew 14:22–31).

How often have we been afraid? How often have we doubted? For that matter, how often have we thought we knew better? Peter, for one, thought nothing of trying to impose his own will over that of Christ's, mistaking his own for the better path.

From that time on, Jesus began to show his disciples that he must go to Jerusalem and undergo great suffering at the hands of the elders and chief priests and scribes, and be killed, and on the third day be raised. And Peter took him aside and began to rebuke him, saying, "God forbid it, Lord! This must never happen to you." But he turned and said to Peter, "Get behind me, Satan! You are a stumbling block to me; for you are setting your mind not on divine things but on human things" (Matthew 16:21–23).

As if these lessons weren't enough to humble Peter, he suffers the indignity of denying Christ not once, not twice, but three times. In other words, Peter strikes out, one, two, three.

Now Peter was sitting outside in the courtyard. A servant-girl came to him and said, "You also were with Jesus the Galilean." But he denied it before all of them, saying, "I do not know what you are talking about." When he went out to the porch, another servant-girl saw him, and she said to the bystanders, "This man was with Jesus of Nazareth." Again he denied it with an oath, "I do not know the man." After a little later the bystanders came up and said to Peter, "Certainly you also are one of them, for your accent betrays you." Then he began to curse, and he swore an oath, "I do not know the man!" At that moment the cock crowed. Then Peter remembered what Jesus had said: "Before the cock crows, you will deny me three times." And he went out and wept bitterly (Matthew 26:69–75).

In a sense it could be said that Peter really *didn't* know the man. Jesus was someone who government authorities viewed as a rebel, and religious leaders saw him as sacrilegious and a threat to their power. Neighbors mocked him, and even his closest associates did not understand his teachings. Here was a man who could heal the sick, give sight to the blind, drive demons out, walk on water, and raise the dead. He also predicted his own death and resurrection three days later! Not your average "Joseph" to say the least. Only when Christ had visited the apostles after his death were all things made clear.

If ever there was a person in the Bible to give us hope, it is Peter: fisherman, brother, husband, well-intentioned follower, headstrong, loyal, weak, faithful, often missing the mark. Peter is a part of us all, a perfect example of what it is to be imperfect, to be human. He fails, and he fails time and again. And Jesus loves him all the more.

Peter was one of the first to realize Jesus was the Messiah. He is called "Satan" for trying to dissuade Jesus from his destiny on the cross. Peter believed so much in Jesus that he asked the Lord to allow him to walk on water. When Christ did so, Peter's own lack of faith caused him to sink. Jesus proclaimed Peter as the rock upon whom he will build his church. Peter denied his Lord three times. Despite all this Jesus forgives Peter, restores him, and believes in him so much he entrusts him with his flock.

Given time, patience and, in some cases, help from above, the veil is lifted, a new day dawns, the Light (of the World) goes on. Teams jell; people come together. Players sacrifice individual goals for the success of the team; people seek to help others, and in so doing help themselves. The game is made easy; life is worth living. The 1962 Mets evolve into the world champion Miracle Mets of '69, not to mention the National League champs of '73. The apostles become the foundation of Christ's Church. They spread the Good News that is Jesus, the Word of God. Simon Peter grows from denying Jesus three times to being the one to whom Christ says, *"You are Peter, and on this rock I will build my church"* (Matthew 16:18).

Of course, happy endings aren't always the case. As humans, we err. As baseball players, we error. We turn away from all that is good in God and the game. We can be spectacular in our failures.

Perhaps the most infamous of all baseball teams was one that actually played in the World Series—the 1919 Chicago White Sox. The year prior, the team objected to the fact that their owner refused to pay to have their uniforms cleaned for several weeks. They even named themselves the Black Sox in protest. That moniker took on a more sinister meaning when it was discovered that eight members of the team had conspired to throw the 1919 World Series against the Cincinnati Reds. The club's top two pitchers, Eddie Cicotte and Claude Williams, as well as their top slugger, Shoeless Joe Jackson, were among those reportedly in on the fix. Judas Iscariot betrayed Jesus for thirty pieces of silver. Four pairs of Sox agreed to a payoff of $100,000—most of which was never seen.

Cicotte and Williams had won fifty-two games between them that season, but both seemed to be mysteriously off the mark in the Series. When word leaked out about the fixed games, baseball itself was in a fix. After one game decided by a Cicotte fielding miscue, Sportswriter Hugh Fullerton wrote:

There is more ugly talk and more suspicion among the fans than there ever has been in any World Series. The rumors of crookedness, of fixed games, and plots are thick. It is not necessary to dignify them by telling what they are but the sad part is that such suspicion of baseball is so widespread.[3]

Eventually, all eight players were acquitted of any wrongdoing, possibly due to the fact that there was no law in Illinois at the time to say that what they did was illegal. However, newly elected baseball commissioner Kennesaw Mountain Landis banned all of the alleged participants from the game forever.

Perhaps the greatest loss was for the fans themselves. We were denied seeing the full career of Joe Jackson, one of the greatest hitters the game has ever produced. Named Shoeless Joe for once playing in the minors without a pair of shoes because they were too tight, Jackson hit .408 in 1911 and had a lifetime average of .356, third highest of all time. Number one in that category, Ty Cobb, never one to praise opposing players, described Jackson as "the greatest natural hitter I ever saw."[4] Babe Ruth, one of baseball's greatest hitters, patterned his swing after the shoeless one.[5]

Baseball's loss of Jackson's spectacular play was brought to modern light in the book *Shoeless Joe* by W. P. Kinsella, on which the movie *Field of Dreams* was based. In the story, Iowa farmer Ray Kinsella, played by Kevin Costner, responds to the mystical call of "if you build it, he will come." *It* being a baseball field in his cornfield. *He* is assumed to be Joe Jackson. And why not? As author Kinsella has character Kinsella say, "'He hit .375 against the Reds in the 1919 World Series and played errorless ball,' my father would say, scratching his head in wonder. Twelve hits in an eight-game series. And *they* suspended *him*."[6]

But in terms of guilt, remorse or sorrow, none of the Black Sox felt the weight of their actions as did Judas for his betrayal of Christ, for what could compare to giving up the son of God to be crucified?

When Judas, his betrayer, saw that Jesus was condemned, he repented and brought back the thirty pieces of silver to the chief priests and the elders. He said, "I have sinned by betraying innocent blood." But they said, "What is that to us? See to it yourself." Throwing down the pieces of silver in the temple, he departed; and he went and hanged himself (Matthew 27:3–5).

As with Joe Jackson, modern cinema also presents a different interpretation of Judas' trials. In the film, *The Last Temptation of Christ*, Judas is portrayed as a confidante of Jesus, the one apostle strong enough to betray a man he fiercely loves in order to put in motion Christ's trial, crucifixion, and resurrection. Few biblical scholars would accept director Martin Scorcese's version over evangelist Matthew's, but it does raise the point that since none of us were present at the time, we cannot say with certainty what did or did not happen.

One thing though is for certain. Both baseball and the Christian faith were able to survive despite, and in some cases because of, these betrayals. Baseball has managed to overcome gambling, work stoppages, free agency, even the designated hitter rule. Catholicism, a faith founded on Christ's death and resurrection, has endured the Crusades, the Spanish Inquisition, three concurrent popes, sexual promiscuity of its leaders, pedophilia, even reports that God is dead.

There is something of faith and baseball that touches the soul, that forgives human error (even by Red Sox first baseman Bill Buckner in the 1986 World Series), that gives many of us a reason for being, that without faith and baseball, a good amount of joy would be taken from the world.

"BABE SOLD TO YANKEES FOR $100,000"

The Book of Ruth

"You...came to a people that you did not know before."

BOOK OF RUTH

AT FIRST ONE MIGHT THINK IT ODD that a religious parallel could be found with the career of George Herman "Babe" Ruth. After all, his appetite for life was legendary and often by no means exemplary. But was not the Christ child called a babe? Did not the Babe perform godlike feats on the baseball diamond? Did not Luke write, *"This will be a sign to you: you will find a child [a Babe] wrapped in bands of cloth and lying in a manger"* (2:12)? And could not it have been written of Ruth: "...this will be the sign to you: You will find the Babe in rumpled clothes, lying to his manager"? More to the point, both the Bible and baseball have a book of Ruth, and the main characters of each have striking similarities.

While the early books of the Bible feature a number of strong women—Adam's Eve, Abraham's Sarah, Moses' Miriam—the Book of Ruth is one of only two collections (Esther being the other) whose story is predominantly about a woman. The tale in short: After their respective husbands die, Ruth accompanies her mother-in-law Naomi from their homeland of Moab to Judah. There, Ruth is befriended by benevolent landowner Boaz, "a man of great wealth," who eventually takes her as his wife. In the course of the story, Ruth demonstrates love and loyalty to Naomi by leaving her own home to venture to a foreign land. In one of the most poignant passages of the Old Testament, Ruth declares her fidelity to her mother-in-law:

> *"Do not press me to leave you,*
> *or to turn back from following you!*
> *Where you go, I will go;*
> *where you lodge, I will lodge;*
> *your people shall be my people,*
> *and your God my God.*
> *Where you die, I will die—*
> *there will I be buried.*
> *May the* LORD *do thus and so to me,*
> *and more as well,*
> *if even death parts me from you!"* (Ruth 1:16–17).

Though Ruth and Naomi migrated to Judah, they did not leave their troubles behind. Being without husbands, they were also without property or protection, living hand to mouth from whatever they could glean from public patches of barley fields. Even when Boaz favored Ruth because she had shown "loyal love" to Naomi, their engagement was in jeopardy.

Just as prior to 1947 blacks were denied the chance to play in the major leagues, Jewish women were forbidden to own property. In what sounds more like a business transaction than a rite of courtship, Jewish law dictated that a male relative close to Ruth had the right of first refusal to take her hand in marriage. This was done so that her husband's land might properly pass to a male heir. The relative had the option to purchase the property, but to do so would obligate him to also marry Ruth. Fortunately, the man declined this right of redemption. And in a biblical fairy tale ending, Ruth and Boaz lived happily ever after, raising a son, Obed, who became the grandfather of King David, from whose lineage Jesus is descended.

So goes the tale of Ruth, as in the Babe. Born George Herman,

Jr., in Baltimore on February 6, 1895, Ruth was separated from his family as was his biblical "cousin." Bouts of theft, hooliganism, and fighting caused his parents to deem him incorrigible. Thus, he was sent to St. Mary's Industrial School for Boys, a combination reform school and orphanage. There he stayed until age eighteen with rarely a visit from his parents. Just as Boaz found favor with his Ruth, so too did the school's disciplinarian with the Babe. Brother Matthias inspired young George to give the game of baseball a try. Ruth proved to be so adept at all aspects of the game that he consistently played on teams four years beyond his age group.

In 1914, the minor league Baltimore Orioles signed the St. Mary's phenom and a year later he was under contract with the Boston Red Sox as a pitcher. As Ward and Burns recount:

> He had only rarely been outside St. Mary's, and everything was new and exciting. "When they let him out," a teammate recalled, "it was like turning a wild animal out of a cage." He wanted to go everywhere, see everything, do everything. He used other people's toothbrushes, ran the elevator up and down, and got married to Helen Woodford, a sixteen-year-old coffee shop waitress he met on his very first day in Boston.
>
> He was bigger, louder, more excitable than his teammates. They called him "Baby," then Babe.[1]

On the baseball field, Ruth did anything but take baby steps. He was part of three Red Sox World Series winners in four years. In the fall classics of 1916 and 1918, he helped pitch the Sox to the titles, winning three games, including the longest complete game victory in World Series history, a 14-inning affair against Brooklyn. In the course of those appearances, he put together a string of 29–2/3 scoreless innings, a mark that would stand for forty-three years. In his first six seasons with the team, he won 89 games, leading the American League in complete games once, shutouts once, and ERA once. In 1919, the Babe moved to outfield and hit 29 home runs, the record for the major leagues at that time, and still managed to chip in with nine victories from the mound.

Yet, as with his biblical namesake, he would be forced to leave his (baseball) family and journey to a strange and distant land—New York City. In what is considered to be the worst transaction in the history of the game, Ruth was sold to the Yankees in 1920, as Red Sox owner Harry Frazee needed cash to offset losses from his baseball and theatrical investments. That he eventually backed a winner, *No, No Nanette*, five years later has been cause for Red Sox rooters ever since to mourn "No, No Harry!" for the owner's shortsighted deal. While the Sox have managed to play in the World Series a handful of times since the trade, they were hapless losers until the 2004 series sweep against St. Louis. So drastic were the fortunes of Boston teams that the Red Sox futile quest for a world championship had been referred to as the "Curse of Babe Ruth."

Even the casual baseball fan is familiar with the exploits of the Babe as a Yankee. Home run champion twelve times, RBI champion six times, batting champion once. He led New York to seven American League pennants and four world championships, including their first. He finished his career with a lifetime batting average of .342, 94 regular season victories as a pitcher, and, of course, 714 home runs, including the long-standing record 60 he hit in 1927.

However, all was not champagne and championships for Ruth. He too had his bouts of misery, of wandering in the desert. In 1922, Commissioner Landis suspended the slugger for 39 games for barnstorming between seasons against the commissioner's instructions. Ruth was suspended twice more during the season for "vulgar and vicious"[2] language to an umpire. All total, the Babe missed almost one third of the year; his power numbers falling from 59 home runs to 35. To make matters worse, the Yankees dropped the World Series to the crosstown Giants in five games. During a postseason dinner, future mayor Jimmy Walker lambasted Ruth for letting down the "dirty-faced kids"[3] who looked up to him.

Embarrassed, hurt and tearful, Ruth vowed to come back even better than before. He lost twenty pounds working on his farm and rededicated himself to the game. In 1923, he led the league in home runs with 41 and RBIs with 131, batted a career-best .393, and even stole 17 bases. To Yankee fans' delight, he led the team to their first world title, a 4–2 Series triumph over the rival Giants.

One might think that the Babe had learned his lesson with his fall from, and subsequent re-ascent of, the mountaintop. However, old habits die hard, especially when temptation is everywhere. Ruth's appreciation of eating, drinking, and the fairer sex finally got the better of him before the 1925 season. So much so that during spring training he collapsed with stomach pain and was rushed to the hospital with an intestinal abscess. The press referred to the ailment as the "bellyache heard round the world."[4]

Now abscess may make the heart grow fonder for the game, but it did nothing for the Babe's timing or temperament. He missed the first two months of the season, then later was fined and suspended for arriving late for a game in August. His batting average dropped by 88 points and his home run total was 21 short of the previous year's. Without the Babe's usual numbers, the Yankees finished in seventh place just two years after winning the Series.

For Babe, if there was a lesson to be learned, it was that if he came back from the abyss once, he could do it again. That he did. Forty-seven homers, 146 RBIs, a .372 average and an American League pennant in 1926. The following year was even better: an unheard of 60 home runs, 164 RBIs and a .356 batting average. He and Lou Gehrig anchored the Yankees' famed Murderer's Row and led what many believe was the best team ever to play the game to a 4–0 sweep of the Pirates in the 1927 Series.

So legendary was the Babe's game that fans by the tens of thousands flocked to the ballparks to see him play. His face adorned magazine covers and cereal boxes. He was headline news whether he ate hot dogs or hit home runs, visited a hospital or a whorehouse. To capitalize on Ruth's popularity, in 1923 the New York team moved into a new home—the majestic Yankee Stadium. To this day, it is referred to as "The House that Ruth Built."

Which leads us to another biblical similarity. As was mentioned earlier, Jesus indeed fulfilled Old Testament prophecy by being born of the House of David. Working our way back down the family tree we find that David was born of the house of Jesse, who was born of the house of Obed, who was born of the house of Boaz, who was married to Ruth. Thus, one could say that Jesus is also from the House of Ruth.

Likewise, the baseball House of Ruth has produced its own legacy. Ruth begot Gehrig who begot DiMaggio who begot Mantle, Ford and Berra who begot Jackson, Hunter, and Munson, who begot Jeter, Williams, and Clemens. These and other Yankee greats have helped New York claim twenty-six world championships, more than double that of their nearest rival.

What is more important, however, than a coincidental sameness of names, and the subsequent strong or weak parallels they provide, is the fact that God brings about great works through the lowly and exalted. Baseball's Ruth was an incorrigible orphan, uneducated, unrefined, and a well-known carouser. But by the accuracy of his arm and power of his bat, he brought glory to two storied franchises, placed the game on his shoulders, and brought its excitement to the masses in a large, even mythical way that no one has equaled before or since.

Biblical Ruth was a woman in a male-dominated culture, a Moabitess in the land of Judah, husbandless, poor and without prospects. Yet through her love for and loyalty to her mother-in-law Naomi, she found favor with Boaz, became his wife and the great-grandmother of David, out of whose house came a carpenter's son, Jesus Christ, the savior of the world.

"WHERE HAVE YOU GONE, JOE DIMAGGIO?"

From the song Mrs. Robinson,
words and music by Paul Simon[1]

And they took Joseph to Egypt.

GENESIS 37:28

GENESIS IS THE SOURCE OF A STORY ABOUT ENVY, betrayal, abandonment, exile, triumph, and reconciliation. In the tale of Joseph and his brothers, these themes collide like the many colors of his tunic. Joseph, son of Jacob, the eleventh of twelve brothers, was somewhat of a braggart (perhaps innocent, perhaps not) as a child. He had the ability to interpret dreams, one of which he explained to his brothers: *"Look, I have had another dream: the sun, the moon, and eleven stars were bowing down to me"* (Genesis 37:9). Hmm? Joseph saw eleven stars; Joseph had eleven brothers. Can you spell "sibling rivalry"?

To teach Joseph a lesson, the brothers cast him down in a pit to die. Realizing this to be a wasted opportunity, they then decided to sell Joseph to a band of wandering traders for twenty shekels of silver. While Joseph was being taken to Egypt as a slave, the brothers rubbed his coat of many colors with blood, then proclaimed him "dead" to their father Jacob. In a truly ironic reversal, just as Jacob earned his birthright through deception, so too did he lose a son.

In Egypt, Joseph was sold to an official of the royal court, where he was soon made overseer of the officer's estate. Not only was Joseph astute, he was *handsome and good-looking* (Genesis 39:6), so much so that the official's wife saw Joseph as a potential boy toy. Having rebuffed the wife's advances, Joseph was wrongly thrown in prison.

Eventually, Joseph's interpretive skills came in to play again. Learning of Joseph's prowess at understanding dreams, the Pharaoh called on the Israelite to shed light on his own troubling visions.

There will come seven years of great plenty throughout all the land of Egypt. After them there will arise seven years of famine, and all the plenty will be forgotten in the land of Egypt; the famine will consume the land (Genesis 41:29–30).

Joseph advised the Pharaoh to stock up during times of plenty. As a show of gratitude, and realizing that God was with the interpreter, Pharaoh gave Joseph the keys to his kingdom, naming him second in command. Said Pharaoh to his servants, *"Can we find anyone else like this?"* (Genesis 41:38).

In his position in Pharaoh's court, Joseph amassed great power and wealth. When famine did strike the land, Egypt was prepared. Not so the land of Jacob, who sent his sons to the south to buy provisions. Joseph encountered the brothers in his court, and after a series of deceptions on Joseph's part, as well as redemption on the brothers', the family was reunited amid tears of joy. Once again, what man (through the brothers' envy) tore apart, God (through his servant Joseph) had brought back together.

Baseball's most famous Joseph also had somewhat similar experiences. Joseph DiMaggio grew up in San Francisco, honing his game on the city sandlots and amateur teams. As a nineteen-year-old, playing for the San Francisco Seals in the Pacific Coast League, DiMaggio hit consecutively in 61 straight games, a record which still stands. After three years with the Seals, DiMaggio was purchased by the New York Yankees. In 1936, the new Yankee outfielder also showed a mastery of his surroundings. He hit .323 in his first year in the bigs, and scored 132 runs, an American League rookie record. DiMaggio continued his ascent, leading the league in home runs and runs scored the following year; winning the batting title and his first Most Valuable Player award the year after that. In 1940, Joltin' Joe added a second batting crown. His first RBI title came in 1941, the year he obliterated the record for consecutive games with a hit, reaching base safely in 56 straight. Even though Ted Williams led the American League with an astounding .406 average that year, DiMaggio was named MVP.

Baseball Joseph's "imprisonment" came during his years in the military during the 1943–45 seasons. In 1946, a foot injury hampered his performance as he batted below .300 for the first time in his career and failed to reach at least 100 RBIs. His "release" came the following year when he captured his third MVP award.

Can we find anyone else like this, indeed? DiMaggio stands out as one of the all-time greats. A baseball best hitting streak, two home run titles, two RBI crowns, back-to-back seasons leading the league in hitting. His play in the field was so effortless that he seemed to glide to fly balls. He was an All-Star in each of his thirteen years in the league. Above all else, he was a champion. By comparison, Babe Ruth, in his fifteen years as a Yankee, won seven pennants and four World Series titles. DiMaggio played on ten pennant winners and nine world champions.

Not surprisingly, the sun, the moon, and the stars bowed down before the Yankee Clipper. He was the toast of New York, and any other town he happened to grace. Tables in the finest restaurants were reserved for him, tickets to the hottest shows were never scarce should he care to attend. One particular star captivated by this "handsome and good-looking" man was Marilyn Monroe. Theirs was a romance for the ages, far eclipsing the likes of Michael Douglas and Catherine Zeta-Jones or Brad Pitt and Jennifer Aniston. Their marriage and subsequent divorce provided DiMaggio his greatest joy and deepest sadness. As biblical Joseph went from slave to overseer to prison to riches, so too did Joltin' Joe ride his own roller coaster of fame and fortune...and sorrow.

DiMaggio was not without his own sibling issues either. His brothers Vince and Dom also left San Francisco to play major league baseball, Vince for five teams in the National League, Dom for eleven seasons with the Boston Red Sox. Dom and Joe even shared All-Star status on several occasions. However, when Dom made a nice catch on a ball hit by his Yankee brother, Joe took it personally. So much so that their relationship became strained for the rest of their lives. In fact, Joe DiMaggio, in his quest for privacy, distanced himself from much of the world.

After biblical Joseph had reunited his family, the Israelites became dependent upon Egyptian resources to survive, eventually leading to their enslavement by the Pharaoh of Moses' time. In Bill Moyers' book *Genesis*, commentator Seyyed Hossein Nasr states that, "too much success in the world will lead to enslavement."[2] For the tribes of Israel, it was enslavement by the Egyptians. Joe DiMaggio became a prisoner of his own solitude.

The Yankees even had their own form of feast and famine. From 1936, DiMaggio's first with the club, through 1964, the New Yorkers appeared in twenty-two World Series, claiming the crown sixteen times. Their fans then had to endure a title drought of twelve years before another appearance in the fall classic, and fifteen years before another world championship.

Both Josephs were blessed with unique gifts, one for prophecy, the ability to see God in the everyday; the other with the skills to hit and catch a baseball like few before or since. Yet even with their gifts they were not immune to the ups and downs, joys and sorrows, of life. Not surprisingly, none of us are. But the constant for each of us is that no matter if we are happy or sad, have hit a home run or struck out, have a surplus of riches or are in need, God is with us. His love for us does not depend on our wealth or health, our fame or our game.

Nor should our love for him.

Bottom of the 3rd
"162 GAMES"
A major league baseball season

For everything there is a season.

ECCLESIASTES 3:1

REFERENCES TO OUR NATIONAL PASTIME abound in Scripture, from predictions to rules of the game, from commentary to play by play. A partial examination of relevant passages of the Bible gives new meaning to the phrase "playing the game by the Book."

Genesis, the first book of the Bible and of the Torah, deals chiefly with the origin of the universe, Adam and Eve, Cain and Abel, Noah and the Ark, Abraham and his descendants all the way through Joseph and his coat of many colors. Yet from its early pages also come the first referrals to the game of baseball.

"Let there be light" (Genesis 1:3). With this command, God illuminated the cosmos. And provided the marching orders for night baseball. Thus, on the evening of May 24, 1935, President Franklin Delano Roosevelt pushed a button in Washington, DC, that lit up Crosley Field some five hundred miles away, allowing the hometown Cincinnati Reds take on the Philadelphia Phillies in baseball's first game under the lights.[1]

But when God gave us light, he had more in mind than just night baseball. He gave us illumination. To understand. To see the light. How often have pitchers struggled early in their careers before having the physical and mental aspects of their games fall into place? For the first five years of his career, Randy Johnson was only one game over .500. It wasn't until he sought advice from fellow fireballer

Nolan Ryan that he became one of the most dominating pitchers in the game. What Johnson is to speed, fellow southpaw Jamie Moyer is to craftiness. *Not* blessed with a live arm, Moyer was twenty games under .500 for his first six seasons. As a student of the game, however, he learned how to turn this seeming liability into an asset. By keeping batters off balance with an assortment of slow offerings, Moyer makes his fastball appear quicker than it really is. At age thirty-nine he became a twenty-game winner for the first time. One year later he made his first All-Star team; two years later he became one of only four pitchers over forty years old to win twenty games.

So too is it with we non-baseball playing Homo sapiens. We struggle with love and life until one day a light goes on. We learn what it is to be a better parent, to relate better to our folks, to appreciate our spouse, to hit a three wood, to set the VCR to record, to keep a soufflé from falling, to see God in our everyday lives.

"Cover it inside and out with pitch" (Genesis 6:14). True, this was an instruction to Noah on how to waterproof the Ark for forty days and nights of rain. But it was also the introduction of pitching strategy. For the best results one should paint the inside and outside corners of the plate, not to mention go high and low in the strike zone. With fastballs and sliders, curves and changeups, split-fingers and knuckleballs. By way of baseball, God also instructs us how to approach life. We are to use all the pitches or talents he has given us. Practice. Hone our skills. Experiment in different areas. Have a game plan and stick to it, yet be willing to improvise. We are to enjoy the variety that life presents us, inside and outside of home, to look for God in the highs and lows that we encounter.

"How awesome is this place!" (Genesis 28:17). Resting from his travels one night, Jacob lay down to sleep and had an amazing dream—angels were ascending and descending a ladder from the earth to the heavens. Upon waking, Jacob declared that the ground must be sacred because God dwelt there. "Awesome" describes the place of Jacob's Ladder as well as a number of baseball's holy

places, including Boston's Fenway Park with the "Green Monster" looming in left field; Wrigley Field in Chicago with its ivy-covered walls; and Yankee Stadium, the House that Ruth built. Some of the newer ballparks are awesome, such as Safeco Field, the diamond of the Seattle Mariners—considered by local fans to be the jewel of the Pacific Northwest; and SBC Park, home of the Giants and wondrous views of the San Francisco skyline and Bay Bridge.

For a baseball fan, to walk into any of these "cathedrals" is a pilgrimage. We honor the great players and wondrous games that have come before. I have had my breath taken away in these ballparks. What causes such a reaction to the physical grandeur of these human-built stadiums? It's to finally be in the presence of something you have heard about, read about, seen pictures of, even loved as a child. It's to be a part of something bigger than that day's particular game, to be a part of the vast tapestry of the "Game" itself. As with the Grand Canyon or the Milky Way, something touches us deep inside, awe for such beauty and power, gratitude for such grandeur and grace. At some level, we are aware that we are in the presence of something larger than ourselves that can only be explained as God.

Following Genesis, the Book of Exodus tells the story of Moses leading the Israelites from captivity in Egypt. Adventures include the parting of the Red Sea (actually the Sea of Reeds), the encounter with God as a burning bush, the presentation of the Ten Commandments, the miracle of manna in the desert, the building of the Ark of the Covenant (given twentieth-century interest thanks to *Indiana Jones* movies), and general wanderings in the wilderness. With all these goings on, it's no wonder that few scholars have pondered the foundations of the game of baseball hidden within the Exodus.

"Strike the rock" (Exodus 17:6). This was God's instruction to Moses as to how to bring water to the thirsty people wandering in the desert so that they might drink. Just as water is fundamental to life, this phrase is the key to the game of baseball. A baseball is often referred to as the Pill, or the Rock. Strike the rock easily becomes

strike at the ball. In other words, batters everywhere are urged to swing away.

When Moses struck the rock, he brought water to the people. Water has also been brought to the game providing fans beauty, majesty and, at times, relief. Kansas City has its fountains in the outfield; San Francisco has McCovey Cove, adding a great deal more drama to any number of Barry Bonds home runs. From its upper promenade, Safeco Field has expansive views of Elliot Bay. The BOB (Bank One Ballpark) in Phoenix offers fans a swimming pool to cool off in, while old Comiskey had a shower that did the same. Infields are watered down before and during the game; managers pause and reflect while taking a trip to the water cooler.

More importantly, baseball also quenches a thirst we have as a people: The common urge to come together as a community for a single purpose. As a country, America rallied around the victims of the 9/11 tragedy and, while there may have been disagreements on how we decided to combat terrorism, Americans fully support our troops. But in everyday life, we have a difficult time agreeing on the best way to allocate our Federal budget. Racial tensions can still be found in this country a century after the Emancipation Proclamation and decades after desegregation. There are still homeless on the streets in a land of plenty. Divisions can be found in most any community, from city council conference tables to street corners. Yet we can all come together on summer evenings in cities all across the country to enjoy the cool night air and marvel over emerald green pastures of outfield grass. We stand together for the national anthem. We cheer as one for the key strikeout or the home run. We all sing baseball's anthem *Take Me Out to the Ball Game* during the seventh inning stretch. There is a shared experience, a unity in faith over the exploits of the twenty-five players wearing our hometown whites, rejoicing with one another in victory, comforting one another in defeat. It is like a community of faithful responds to a couple joined in marriage or a family experiencing the death of a loved one. In baseball and faith, it is as community that we all come together.

In Numbers, the fourth book of the Bible and Torah, the Israelites approach the Promised Land, though only Joshua and Caleb of the original wanderers, those who took part in the Exodus from Egypt, actually cross over to Canaan. And like the establishment of franchises in cities for the first National League, the twelve tribes receive instructions on how to disperse into the land.

"Is the LORD's power limited?" (Numbers 11:23). This is God's rhetorical question to Moses when the latter questioned the Almighty's power to provide meat for the entire people of the Exodus. It is also a statement about the finite nature of a baseball career and of life itself.

As much as the game is played by the young at heart, there comes a day when every ballplayer's power is limited. Careers are cut short from injury or eventually end due to ineffectiveness. In 1957, Herb Score, a promising Cleveland Indians pitcher, had his career come to a premature end as a result of a line drive taken in the head one season after winning twenty games and two seasons after being named American League Rookie of the Year. Mark "the Bird" Fidrych captivated the country with his fanciful antics on the mound and by talking to the ball. Unfortunately, arm troubles plagued him after a brilliant 19-win rookie season in 1976. Pittsburgh Pirate Steve Blass, the World Series hero of 1971, inexplicably could not locate home plate two years later, retiring for good in 1974. Cardinal left-hander Rick Ankiel had a very wild appearance in the 2001 playoffs and is now trying to make a comeback as an outfielder. Steve Sax of the Dodgers and Chuck Knoblauch of the Yankees had trouble making routine throws from second base to first. Promising catcher Mike Ivie could not make the throw back to the pitcher without double clutching, causing him to move to third base. In 1989, Giant left-hander Dave Dravecky had a severe power limitation. After an inspirational comeback from cancer, his arm snapped in two after throwing a pitch. His arm was eventually amputated. Hall of Fame pitcher Steve "Lefty" Carlton, winner of 329 games in his career, was unable to comprehend his declining power late in his career, going 16–37 during his last four seasons. Similarly, Warren Spahn, the all-time winningest left-hander in history with 363 victories, went 13–29 in his last two campaigns.

Though God-given, our talents do not last forever. We can no longer catch up to the fastball; our memory fails us. We're a step slower on the bases; we have to walk with a cane. Part of playing the game is to accept the day when we have exhausted our talents. Part of living life is to accept age, frailty, even dying. We pass our legacy onto our children and grandchildren, just as new ballplayers take the place of old. All of which serves in stark contrast to God's question to Moses, "Is the Lord's power limited?" Our abilities, bodies, and minds may fail us, but God's arm never does. His love for us, his mercy for us, are everlasting.

At first, one might not think to find anything but uprightness in the Bible and fair play in baseball. But both are full of surprises. Samuel 1 and 2 treat us to stories of political and sexual intrigue.

Take David for example. Hand selected by Samuel to become King of Israel. Slayer of Goliath. Author of some of the most poignant and beautiful psalms in the Bible. Father of Solomon. Ancestor of Jesus. Pretty impressive resumé. Of course his story's not complete without mention of the fact that he sent a solider, Uriah the Hittite, to his death in battle to cover the fact that he had impregnated the man's wife, Bathsheba.

Now take Wade Boggs. Five-time American League batting champion. Member of the exclusive 3,000-hit club, twelve-time All-Star. Member of the 1996 world champion New York Yankees. Husband and, by the way, philanderer, having maintained a lengthy relationship with Margo Adams during his playing days in Boston.

Then there's the pitching pair of Fritz Peterson and Mike Kekich. Peterson was a 20-game winner in 1970, while Kekich had back-to-

-back 10-win seasons in 1971–1972. In something straight out of the movie *Bob and Carol and Ted and Alice,* Kekich and Peterson not only switched wives, but they switched families—kids, houses, and pets included. Needless to say, neither pitcher's career, or life, was the same. It may be inconsequential to mention, but both were left-handed and both played for the Yankees at the time.

David's tryst with Bathsheba, Moses killing an Egyptian overseer, Peter denying Jesus three times; Babe Ruth's womanizing, Mickey Mantle's drinking, Pete Rose's gambling, the Bible and baseball are filled with tales of people acting very unsaintly, but that's the point. We are all human, from the people who populated the Sea of Galilee to those who take residence in the fields of baseball. We are not perfect, yet out of our imperfections come great things. Babe Ruth's exploits inspired the building of Yankee Stadium. Mickey Mantle became the greatest switch-hitter to ever play. Pete Rose collected the most hits in the history of the game. Moses led the Israelites out of captivity. David wrote the Book of Psalms. Peter became the first leader of the Church. Even with our own imperfections we are capable of good things, from helping the elderly to serving on a school board to reading a story to our children at night.

Chronicles 1 and 2 do not refer to the San Francisco and Houston newspapers. They are the books of the Christian Bible that follow the Book of Kings. In the Hebrew Bible, they come at the end of Scriptures. Chronicles could have just as easily have been called Recapitulations. Written approximately when the Jewish people returned from captivity in Babylon, Chronicles seeks to give the Israelites renewed hope in their covenant as the chosen people of God. Thus follows a shortened, and often sanitized, version of Jewish history. It includes the genealogies of the twelve tribes, the life and death of King David, a revisit to Solomon's temple, a chronicle of the twenty rulers of Judah, and a summary of the exile in Babylon. Sort of like a history of the New York Yankees minus Ruth's womanizing, Mantle's drinking, and Billy Martin's legendary temper.

Pure gold...basins [pitchers] (1 Chronicles 28:17). This is part of a lengthy description of the ornate articles of service to be included in the vestibule of the temple of Solomon, as passed on by King David to his son.

One doesn't need to be as wise as Solomon to realize that it's also a fairly accurate description of the golden armed pitchers of the 1960s and 1970s. Southpaw Sandy Koufax dominated the National League from 1962 until his retirement after the 1966 season. Koufax averaged 22 wins a season in those five years, leading the league in earned run average in each year. Along the way he threw four no-hitters including one perfect game, and earned three Cy Young Awards. If Koufax was considered pitcher Number One, then San Francisco Giant ace Juan Marichal was Number One A. What Koufax did with his left hand, Marichal virtually matched with his right. From 1963 through 1969, the Dominican Dandy posted six seasons of 20 wins or more, three with 25 or more. Another tremendous National League hurler of this era was Bob Gibson, one of the most intimidating and competitive pitchers ever to play the game. Gibson led the St. Louis Cardinals to four pennants in the '60s (1963, 1964, 1967, and 1968) and two world championships. His astounding 1.12 ERA in 1968 was the lowest since Walter Johnson set his 1.09 mark fifty-five years earlier. That same year Gibson won the National League's MVP and Cy Young Awards.

Leading the way through the 1970s were Ferguson Jenkins and Jim Palmer. Jenkins, playing for usually less than stellar Chicago Cub teams, hurled his way to seven seasons of 20 or more wins, including six in a row from 1967 through 1972, picking up a Cy Young Award of his own. Palmer, for his part, owned the American League from 1970 through 1978, with eight seasons of at least twenty victories as a member of the Baltimore Orioles. He also seemed to own the Cy Young Award, being voted the best pitcher in the American League three times.

Written as poems to be sung in praise or lamented in sorrow, the

Book of Psalms expresses the full range of human emotions. The 150 prayerful poems that comprise the psalms feature desperate cries of despair, confessions of wrongdoing, and joyful praise for God the Creator, Comforter and Provider, as well as many reverential references to, believe it or not, baseball. Baseball too has inspired songs of praise and poems of lament. Terry Cashman paid tribute to Willie Mays, Mickey Mantle, and the Duke (Snider) in *Talking Baseball*. Paul Stookey of Peter, Paul, and Mary sang of redemption playing *Rightfield*. John Fogerty hoped that his coach would put him in to play *Centerfield*. Millions of fans sing *Take Me Out to the Ball Game* every year. No doubt as many have ridden the roller coaster of hope and despair while reading the poem *Casey at the Bat*.

The work of your fingers (Psalm 8:3). This Psalm of King David rejoices at the work of God's fingers, creating the moon and the stars, and making man nearly the equal of angels.

David just as easily could have been singing the praises of relief pitcher extraordinaire Rollie Fingers. With a throwback handlebar moustache, Fingers had 341 saves in his seventeen-year career, number six all-time. He piled up over 1,500 innings coming out of the bullpen, fourth most in major league history, as well as 114 wins, the fourth most for a reliever. As the supreme protector of late game leads, Fingers helped the Oakland A's close the door on the rest of baseball, taking three world championships in a row from 1972 through 1974.

"The work of your fingers,"…Might David have been referring to the work of fingers in baseball, from the grips of the different pitches to fingers wrapping the handle of the bat, from the design of baseball gloves to the flashing of signs from third base? Even the making of bats, balls, and gloves involves the fingers of workers all around the world. On a larger scale, while playing the game requires us to hold a baseball with our fingers, many of us hold baseball in our hearts.

Even though I walk through the darkest valley, I fear no evil (Psalm 23:4–5). This verse is from the Twenty-Third Psalm, one of the most well known in Scripture, oft quoted for its comforting images of God's protection and love. Here it is in its entirety:

> *The Lord is my shepherd; I shall not want.*
>   *He makes me lie down in green pastures;*
> *he leads me beside still waters;*
>   *he restores my soul.*
> *He leads me in right paths*
>   *for his name's sake.*

> *Even though I walk through the darkest valley,*
>   *I fear no evil;*
> *for you are with me;*
>   *your rod and your staff—*
> *they comfort me.*

> *You prepare a table before me*
>   *in the presence of my enemies;*
> *you anoint my head with oil;*
>   *my cup overflows.*
> *Surely goodness and mercy shall follow me*
>   *all the days of my life,*
> *and I shall dwell in the house of the Lord*
>   *my whole life long.*

To face danger, even death, and fear no evil requires composure that can only come from above. Perhaps this is the same sort of comfort New York Giant left-hander Carl Hubbell had when he faced five of the most feared sluggers in baseball during the 1934 All-Star game. By mastering the screwball, a sort of reverse curve, King Carl recorded five consecutive seasons of at least twenty-one victories from 1933 through 1937. One of the finest moments of his career came in the 1934 contest between greats from the National and

American leagues. Hubbell fanned Lou Gehrig and Babe Ruth of the Yankees, Jimmie Foxx of the A's, Al Simmons of the White Sox, and Joe Cronin of the Senators. Famed sportswriter Paul Gallico wrote:

> By that time Hubbell's magic had become too potent. It filmed Foxx's eye and slowed his muscles. The old dipsie doodle ball was swooping and dipping. There was red-hot magic on it. It was turning into a rabbit, or a humming bird, or a bunch of flowers on its way to the plate. It would come up in front of Foxx's eyes and then vanish completely. Foxx struck out swinging. The crowd lifted the Polo Grounds six feet off the ground with a roar and then set it down again.[2]

Five American League All-Stars. Five legends in their own right. Five eventual members of the Baseball Hall of Fame. And Carl Hubbell walked into the darkest valley of sure baseball death and feared no evil. As for the rest of the non-screwball throwing race, whatever obstacles we encounter or struggles we endure, we have the tools to safely see us through on our journey, from untapped reserves of strength in the face of adversity to the comfort that faith provides in times of despair.

Let the field exult, and everything in it (Psalm 96:12). In the Ninety-Sixth Psalm, voices are raised in praise to the Lord God who shall come in glory and judgment. Oh, what a wonderful expression this particular verse. Ask any major leaguer, they are truly thankful to be blessed with the talent and abilities to play baseball. Watch any child in the stands, hat on head, mitt in hand, and you will see pure unadulterated joy. Baseball is our security blanket, providing comfort in good times and bad. Whether our country is going through the depression of the 1930s or is suffering from the aftermath of Hurricane Katrina, watching our sons and daughters go off to World War II or our friends and neighbors go off to fight in Iraq, baseball has been there, offering continuity and community, comfort and joy.

Isaiah is one of the most prolific writers of Scripture. An advisor to four kings of Judah, Isaiah exhorted the Israelites to mend their wicked ways or face disastrous consequences. At the same time, Isaiah spoke of promise and hope, predicting that one day a Messiah would bring comfort and joy to the chosen people.

> *For a child has been born for us,*
> *a son given to us;*
> *authority rests upon his shoulders;*
> *and he is named*
> *Wonderful Counselor, Mighty God,*
> *Everlasting Father, Prince of Peace* (Isaiah 9:6).

Anyone familiar with the composer George Frideric Handel's majestic *Messiah* will recognize Isaiah's verse as the basis for the lyrics. *And he is named.* Baseball players, too, have had titles bestowed on them as a way for the people to recognize greatness in their midst. George Herman Ruth was known as The Babe, The Bambino, and The Sultan of Swat. Ted Williams was called The Kid, Teddy Ballgame, and The Splendid Splinter. Joe DiMaggio earned the nickname The Yankee Clipper. Willie Mays answered to the Say Hey Kid. And home run king Henry Aaron was called Hammerin' Hank.

A cursory review of any baseball record book might suggest that monikers were the national pastime of the national pastime. You've got your Choo Choo and Big Train; Mookie and Cookie; Doc and Duke; Jiggs and Jocko; Moxie and Mickey; Moose, Goose, Ducky, Chicken and Possum; Mudcat and Catfish; Schoolboy and Showboat; Irish and Dutch; Chippy, Gibby, Gabby, Dusty, Rusty, Putsy, Rocky, Doggie, Cozy, Tubby, Heinie, Pinky, Tiny, Minnie, Wickey, Wiki and Ziggy; Chito, Chico, Chipper, Clipper and Chili; Bing, Biff, Bump, Buddy, Bobo, Buster, Butch, Buzz, Dizzy, Daffy, Sparky, Smoky, Skeeter, Scrappy, Snappy, Stuffy, Skip, Slats, Snooks, Spider, Sport, Specs, Tripp, Topsy, Woody, Whitey, Crash, Red and

Tex; not to mention Peaches, June, Granny, Ginger, Buttercup, Lena, Dot, Sherry, Goldie, Patsy and, lest we forget, Peanuts.

Nicknames offer us an insight into a player's youth. They remove players from the pedestal and make them more accessible in our minds. Nicknames help keep the game young, reminding us that even if grown men are playing, baseball is still a kid's game at heart. Likewise, when we speak of God, it is hard for us to imagine a relationship with the all-powerful, ever-living Creator of all that is. So in our human way, we bestow "nicknames" on God himself. He becomes more knowable and approachable to us. When we pray to our Father, we in effect become children of God. When we refer to Jesus as the Savior of the World, we become the rescued.

With the New Testament come the four gospels. This "good news" is then followed by the Acts of the Apostles, the trials and tribulations of Christ's first followers as recounted by Luke, one of the four evangelists. After Acts come the epistles, letters primarily written by Paul and other leaders of the early Church encouraging new Christian communities that were forming in and around the Mediterranean. Finally comes Revelation, John of Patmos' symbolic and oftentimes difficult to understand account of the Last Day. It is from these writings that we learn of the life of Jesus, and how his death and resurrection have earned us a seat in the kingdom of God the Father. We are instructed how to live our lives in right relationship with God and one another.

"The field is the world" (Matthew 13:38). In the thirteenth chapter of Matthew, the disciples asked Jesus to explain the parable of the wheat and the tares to them. Tares closely resemble wheat but are poisonous to human beings. Only when the final fruit appears can a farmer tell tares from wheat. Thus, both wheat and tares coexist until the time for harvest, much like good and evil, or believers and nonbelievers, exist in our world until Jesus returns on the last day.

As for baseball, everything we learn on the field teaches us about the world. How to handle success and failure, how to overcome adversity, how to get along with your teammates (neighbors), working toward a common goal, wasting or developing talents, how brief a career (read life) really is, passing on what you know to those who follow, labor and management relations, patience, joy, heartbreak, friendship, and love. Is this a great game or what?

"There will be earthquakes" (Mark 13:8). In Mark's thirteenth chapter, Jesus referred to events that will take place on earth before the Last Day and the Second Coming of Christ. Though there will be conflicts between nations and natural disasters, the Gospel will spread through the entire world, making way for the Lord and eventual salvation for those who believe. But before all this would occur, there will be earthquakes in various places.

Not only did Mark concern himself about the life of Jesus, he certainly had an eye toward postseason play. Is there any question that this verse predicted the 1989 World Series between the Oakland A's and the San Francisco Giants? The Play by the Bay, the first ever San Francisco Bay Area World Series, pitted Oakland's Bash Brothers of Jose Canseco and Mark McGwire against the Giant power plant of National League MVP Kevin Mitchell and Will Clark. The A's also featured playoff-tested veterans such as Rickey Henderson, Dave Stewart, and Dennis Eckersley, while the Giants had, well... Mitchell and Clark. A's pitchers Stewart and Mike Moore limited the Giants to just one run in the first two games, giving Oakland a comfortable two games to none lead.

On October 17, at 5:04 PM, just minutes before the third game's first pitch, an earthquake measuring 7.1 on the Richter Scale rocked San Francisco's Candlestick Park and the entire Bay Area. A deck collapsed on the Bay Bridge, levels of the raised Embarcadero Freeway fell, fires spread in the Marina district. The quake claimed sixty-seven lives. Commissioner Fay Vincent postponed the Series indefinitely. Moved by the wishes of Bay Area residents, Vincent allowed the third game to be played ten days later. Possibly still shaken by the quake, no doubt still in shock after the first two games, the Giants never got untracked as Oakland took games three and four and the World Series. Despite the grandeur of the fall classic, however, baseball had to take a back seat to the power of creation, and of God, as manifested through the shifting of two of the earth's home plates.

"From now on you will be catching people" (Luke 5:10). Luke was an educated man of his time, a physician. He had traveled with Paul on many missionary journeys. By contrast, it is thought that the gospel writer Mark was Peter's "biographer." Each of these evangelists recorded an account of Jesus recruiting two sets of brothers, Simon (Peter) and Andrew, and James and John, as apostles.

After an unsuccessful night of fishing, the four men were returning to the shore. Jesus had climbed into Simon's boat and had preached to a multitude on the shore. When he stopped preaching, he told the fishermen to drop their nets in a particular spot. Simon protested that they had fished all over to no avail. But they did as he requested and their nets were filled to the breaking point. Realizing he was in the presence of a miracle worker, Simon fell to his knees and declared, *"Go away from me, Lord, for I am a sinful man!"* And Jesus said to Simon, *"Do not be afraid, from now on you will be catching people"* (Mark 5:8, 10).

And catch people they did. Peter became the Rock, upon whom Christ built his church. John, the self-described disciple whom Jesus loved, was given the responsibility from the cross of caring for Mary, Jesus' mother. Later it is believed he wrote the gospel that bears his name. James became one of the early martyrs of the faith.

"From now on you will be catching people." Christ might have said those same words to major league catchers Johnny Bench, Yogi Berra, Roy Campanella, Mickey Cochrane, Bill Dickey, Carlton Fisk, Josh Gibson, and Mike Piazza. Combined they caught people such as Whitey Ford, Lefty Gomez, Lefty Grove, Don Gullet, Don Newcombe, Satchel Paige, Johnny Podres, Allie Reynolds, Preacher Roe, Schoolboy Rowe, Red Ruffing, and Luis Tiant. Bench, Berra, Campy, Cochrane, and Dickey helped lead their teams to titles. Fisk

and Piazza helped take theirs to the Series. And Gibson, star in the Negro Leagues, would have had if he ever been given the chance to catch in the bigs. But he played before the so-called color line was broken, before Jackie Robinson.

It is a distinguished group. They hit for average: Cochrane had a lifetime mark of .320, Dickey .313. Piazza set a single-season record for catchers of .362. They hit for power. It was said that Gibson, called the Negro league Babe Ruth, hit more than 800 home runs. Bench led the National League in home runs twice, and he, Berra, and Fisk all hit at least 313 home runs as catchers. They could catch and throw. Each was an All-Star and Bench, Berra, and Campanella earned MVPs, with Yogi and Campy receiving the award three times.

"Blessed is the one who stays awake" (Revelation 16:15). In the Bible, the word *blessed* can also be translated as "happy." Happy are those who stay awake and watch for God, for they shall be rewarded. The same can be said for anyone who stays awake to watch baseball. Joy may be found in a come-from-behind victory by the home team. Or a play in the field worthy of an ESPN Web Gem. Perhaps it's the opportunity to see a future Hall of Fame player such as Barry Bonds or Alex Rodriguez, Randy Johnson or Roger Clemens. Maybe it's a chance to see the next Joe DiMaggio or Bob Gibson. Better still, it might be the opportunity to see the astonishment on your nine-year-old child's face when you help guide a foul ball into his or her oversized glove. Take in a July game and you may be reminded what it was like to play catch with your dad late one summer evening as the sun cast a golden glow on your own field of dreams.

Yes, to be sure, happy are those who stay awake.

For in staying awake, looking, seeing, we find God in us. Jesus presents us with daily opportunities to feed the hungry, clothe the naked, give shelter to the homeless, comfort the afflicted, and give hope to the oppressed. It may be contributing to a soup kitchen, giving clothes to a St. Vincent de Paul outlet, volunteering at a homeless shelter, visiting with a sick friend or relative, or writing letters for

Amnesty International. For Jesus said, *"Truly I tell you, just as you did it to one of the least of these who are members of my family, you did it to me"* (Matthew 25:40).

As we've seen, there are many connections we can make between the Bible and baseball. But perhaps all we really need to know can be found by visiting chapter three of Ecclesiastes. There, we find some of the most beautiful verses in the Bible from which comes a valuable lesson about baseball...and life.

> *For everything there is a season...*
> *a time to seek [gain],*
> *and a time to lose.*
> ECCLESIASTES 3:1, 6

"JACKIE'S GOING TO THE MAJOR LEAGUES!"[1]

Buck O'Neil

...the Gentiles had also accepted the word of God.

ACTS 11:1

FROM THEIR RESPECTIVE HUMBLE BEGINNINGS, baseball and the Catholic faith are now known all over the world. Disciples in both camps run the gamut of zealous follower to passive, detached spectator.

In the 2000 Olympics, baseball was a medal event (with the USA capturing the gold). Teams from more than twenty countries compete every year to play in the Little League World Series, from Panama to the Philippines, Nicaragua to Netherlands Antilles, Taiwan to Turkey.

Catholicism is practiced by almost one billion people, nearly one fifth of the world's population. It is the largest of the Christian faiths. Even in such a bastion of Buddhism as China, one percent of the population is Christian. In India, where four out of every five people practice Hinduism, Christianity has made inroads.

But it wasn't always this way.

From very early on, baseball was referred to as our "national pastime." And despite it being influenced by the English games of rounders and cricket, baseball has long been considered the All-American game. However, while large numbers of Americans may have played baseball in city streets and country fields, the professional game itself was closed to people of color. Sure, black ballplayers could play in their own leagues. They just weren't allowed to play in the "majors." It took decades for the game of baseball to finally allow blacks to play at the highest level.

From the late 1800s until Jackie Robinson of the Brooklyn Dodgers broke the color barrier in 1947, baseball was, as sportswriter Roger Kahn put it, "persistently, defiantly, arrogantly, monochromatic. White."[2] Just as what eventually became Christianity was in its infancy a variation of the Jewish faith.

Baseball drew its color line in 1884 after two black brothers from Ohio, Welday Wilberforce Walker and Moses Fleetwood Walker, played for Toledo in the American Association, which was considered the major leagues at the time. Welday played five games in the outfield; Moses caught 42 games and batted a respectable .263.[3]

As Kahn wrote in an article on Jackie Robinson in Gerald Astor's *The Baseball Hall of Fame 50th Anniversary Book,*

> As far as anyone knows, there was never a written agreement among club owners barring blacks, no reverse Emancipation Proclamation, so to speak. But the discrimination was real and ardent. Baseball was a white man's game. The players were white, the coaches were white, the front office people were white, and all of the sportswriters who chronicled the game were white as the players they described. Blacks... could pay their way in but, it became an article of baseball faith, blacks must never be permitted to play organized ball.[4]

Prejudice even existed within these white ranks, directed at one of the finest players to ever grace the game, two-time Most Valuable Player and Hall of Famer Hank Greenberg. Among his career highlights were leading the Detroit Tigers to two World Series and one championship in 1935. He won the major league home run crown in 1938, hitting 58, two shy of Babe Ruth's single season landmark of 60. Though one of the most feared sluggers of his time (he led the

American League in homers four seasons), the fans did not welcome him with open arms.

Why? Because he was Jewish.

Greenberg was not the first Jewish major leaguer, but because of his prowess at the plate and the anti-Semitism of the time, he became a target of abuse. "There was added pressure of being Jewish," he remembered. "How the hell could you get up to home every day and have some son of a bitch call you a Jew bastard and a kike and a sheeny and get on your ass without feeling the pressure? If the ballplayers weren't doing it, the fans were."[5]

It was hard to tell what endeared Greenberg to Jewish fans more—his majestic home runs or his faith. In 1934, with the Tigers involved in a tight pennant race, Greenberg sought spiritual guidance as to whether he should play on the Jewish holy days of Rosh Hashanah and Yom Kippur. Rabbi Leo Franklin advised that Greenberg should play on Rosh Hashanah, as it was a happy occasion, the Jewish New Year, and pray, not play, on the Day of Atonement, Yom Kippur. Poet Edgar Guest spoke for millions when he wrote:

We shall miss him in the infield and shall miss him at the bat
But he's true to his religion—and I honor him for that.[6]

Even as recently as the 1960s, with perhaps the greatest left-handed pitcher the game has ever known—Sandy Koufax—prejudice against Jewish players was still prevalent. From 1962 through 1966, Koufax was the most dominant hurler in baseball, putting together numbers that boggle the mind: a won-loss record of 111–34 (that's an average of better than 22–7 per year), 33 shutouts, and 1,444 strikeouts in 1,377 innings. He led the league in earned run average five years in a row, led the league in wins, shutouts, and strikeouts three years, and twice led in innings pitched and complete games.

Want more? He pitched no-hitters four years in a row, capping the string with a perfect game in 1965. And led his team to three

National League pennants, and two world championships. At thirty years of age he retired, the victim of a severely arthritic elbow that has left his left arm crooked to this day.

However, before the acclaim and the fame, before the dominance and prominence, Sandy Koufax was as erratic as he was hard throwing. Signed to a bonus in 1955, he was long on potential and short on control. Jane Levy wrote in *Sandy Koufax: A Lefty's Legacy:*

> His guaranteed money—and his guaranteed spot on the major league roster—ensured a cool reception from some teammates.... "Some of the players did not like him because he was a Jew," (Dodger pitching great and African American Don) Newcombe says, "I couldn't understand the narrow-mindedness of these players when they came and talked to *us* (the black players on the team) about Sandy as 'this kike' and 'this Jew bastard' or 'Jew sonofabitch that's gonna take my job.' Players used to complain that he threw the ball too hard. But the way they used to complain—'The wild Jew sonofabitch, I'm not gonna hit against that...'—and they'd use the f word—'...that kike, as wild as he is.'"[7]

But despite the taunts, the abuse, the mental hardship, at least Greenberg and Koufax were able to play the game they loved. Baseball greats (and they were great) from the Negro leagues such as Josh Gibson, Buck Leonard, Buck O'Neil, Cool Papa Bell, Judy Johnson, and countless others were never given that chance. Black Americans were not allowed to play the All-American game.

Were they good enough? In many ways, they put their white counterparts to shame. Organized baseball played station-to-station baseball, that is, base to base, while waiting for a home run. Play in the Negro leagues was far more stylish and aggressive. Steals, hit and runs, bunt and runs, taking the extra base on a hit to the outfield. No doubt there were a good many white ballplayers who were glad of baseball's closed-door policy for it allowed them to keep jobs they might have otherwise lost to better-skilled black ballplayers.

Were the black players really good enough? Cool Papa Bell was said to be the fastest man to ever play the game. In a game against major league all-stars, he scored all the way from first base—on a sacrifice bunt. He was clocked around the bases in *under* thirteen seconds. He was reported to be so fast that a teammate once said, "He could turn off the lights and be in under the covers before the room got dark."[8]

Author of that quote, Satchel Paige, was no slouch himself when it came to throwing the ball. Before breaking into the majors in 1948, Paige estimated that he had won 2,000 games and pitched about 100 no-hitters. Of his debut with the Indians, he said, "I ain't as fast as I used to be. I used to overpower 'em; now I outcute 'em. I used my single windup, my triple windup, my hesitation windup, and my now windup…my step-and-pitch-it, my sidearm throw and my bat dodger."[9] He ended his first season in the major leagues with a 6–1 won-loss record—at the age of forty-two.

Only one player may have matched Satchel's immense popularity in the Negro leagues—Josh Gibson. He has been called "the black Babe Ruth." Those who saw him play no doubt had a different opinion—that Babe was "the white Josh Gibson." His power was legendary. An eyewitness claims he saw Gibson hit a ball out of Yankee Stadium, something that Yankee Hall of Famers Babe Ruth, Lou Gehrig, Joe DiMaggio, Mickey Mantle, or Reggie Jackson never did. Said Roy Campanella, a teammate of Jackie Robinson's on the Dodgers and a veteran of both the Negro and major leagues, "[Gibson was] the greatest player I ever saw."[10] Buck O'Neil, ex-Negro League player, and a baseball man for six decades, echoed that sentiment: "Outstanding hitter. The best hitter that I've ever seen. He had the power of Ruth and the hitting ability of Ted Williams. That was Josh Gibson."[11]

Bell, Paige, Gibson, and more were good enough to play major league baseball. They just weren't white enough. But in 1947, one man changed all that.

Before Hank Aaron, there was Josh Gibson. Before Bob Gibson, there was Satchel Paige. Before Lou Brock, there was Cool Papa Bell. And before Aaron, Gibson, and Brock, before Willie Mays, Ernie Banks, and Frank Robinson, before Reggie Jackson, Barry Bonds, and Ken Griffey, Jr., even before Roberto Clemente, Juan Marichal, and Sammy Sosa, there was Jackie Robinson.

Mr. Robinson's heroic achievement of integrating baseball has been well-chronicled, and deservedly so. Members of his own team circulated a petition stating that they'd rather be traded than play with a black teammate. Yet the *Boston Chronicle* trumpeted "Triumph of Whole Race Seen in Jackie's Debut in Major League Ball."[12]

Black America was overjoyed. New attendance records were set in Chicago, Cincinnati, Philadelphia, and Pittsburgh. People were naming their children after Robinson. At the same time, opposing players and fans reviled him. In a game against Cincinnati, the crowd was so venomous in its taunting of Robinson, that Pee Wee Reese, Dodger shortstop and Kentucky-bred, walked across the infield to his teammate and draped an arm around his shoulder, a simple, heartfelt gesture that spoke volumes far greater than the crowd could muster.

Ward and Burns recall a similar incident:

When the Phillies arrived for a three game series, they began shouting racial epithets during batting practice and kept it up until the last out.... "Nigger, go back to the cotton fields"; "We don't want you here, nigger"; "Hey, snowflake, which one of you white boys' wives are you dating tonight?"... By the third day of this ceaseless abuse, even Eddie Stankey had had all he could take: "Listen you yellow-bellied bastards," he bellowed, "why don't you yell at somebody who can answer back?"[13]

It should be noted that Stankey, a Southerner from Alabama, the man who now sprang to his teammate's defense, had been one of the Dodgers to start the above-mentioned petition. It seems after playing along side his black teammate, Mr. Stankey came to appreciate Robinson for his skills as a player, and empathize with Robinson the man for all he had to endure. Stankey's very real change of heart, proved that conversion is not the sole, or soul, province of Christianity.

Ever so slowly, baseball began to grow up, to overcome certain reprehensible actions and live up to its potential as the All-American game. Pee Wee Reese's gesture not only told the world that Jackie Robinson was his teammate but also his friend. Eddie Stankey's reversal of feelings for his fellow Dodger was an example of how not only the game could change, but people as well. Baseball demonstrated that while we are sometimes slow to realize and learn from our mistakes, eventually we do strive to do what's right, we do try live up to our high ideals.

As the first black ballplayer in major league baseball since 1884, Jackie Robinson was Rookie of the Year in 1947 and Most Valuable Player two years after that. He helped bring a world title to Brooklyn, hit better than .300 for six seasons straight, and retired with a lifetime mark of .311. All this while enduring continual death threats on himself, his wife, and his son. In 1947, Jack Roosevelt Robinson integrated baseball. In 1962, Jack Roosevelt Robinson integrated the Baseball Hall of Fame.

Like baseball, early Christianity was a closed society, too. From the time God made his covenant with Abraham, the Jews believed themselves to be the chosen people. Prophets such as Isaiah predicted the coming of Christ to God's people, with two of the most famous of proclamations being these:

> *"Look, the young woman is with child and*
> *shall bear a son, and shall name him Immanuel"*
> (Isaiah 7:14).

For a child has been born for us,
   a son given to us;...
   and he is named
Wonderful Counselor, Mighty God,
   Everlasting Father, Prince of Peace (Isaiah 9:6).

Kenneth Davis summarizes the relationship between Jesus and the Jews rather neatly:

To the devout Jews who accepted him, Jesus was the promised Savior who fulfilled the promise expressed in their Scriptures of a coming "Messiah" or "anointed one" from the line of David who would deliver the children of Israel and usher into a new age of peace and God's rule.[14]

Jesus was born a Jew, no doubt studied the Torah, taught and preached in the temple. His handpicked followers were Jewish, as were most of those to whom they ministered. As such, the foundations of what eventually became Christianity were decidedly Jewish. In fact, "the way" of the Lord was considered by many to be a small sect within the Jewish faith.

However, it was a woman, and a Gentile at that, who helped influence Jesus to expand his thinking about his mission.

From there he set out and went away to the region of Tyre. He entered a house and did not want anyone to know he was there. Yet he could not escape notice, but a woman whose little daughter had an unclean spirit immediately heard about him, and she came and bowed down at his feet. Now the woman was a Gentile, of Syrophoenician origin. She begged him to cast the demon out of her daughter. He said to her, "Let the children be fed first, for it is not fair to take the children's food and throw it to the dogs." But she answered him, "Sir, even the dogs under the table eat the children's crumbs." Then he said to her, "For saying that, you may go—the demon has left your daughter." So she went home, found the child lying on the bed, and the demon gone (Mark 7:24–30).

In his mind, Jesus' first priority was to minister to his "children," the sheep of Israel. Thus, a Greek woman would not normally command his attention. But through their playful verbal sparring, a remarkable thing happened—a shift in Jesus' thinking, a change of the Lord's heart. All people, Jew and Gentile alike, could benefit from the Word of God.

Given this, it's not all that surprising to find Matthew's Gospel telling of Jesus curing the servant of a Roman centurion, or John's Gospel telling us of Jesus spreading his word to a Samaritan. Both were extremely bold moves. Judea was under Roman rule at the time. In effect, Jesus was opening up his heart to the Jews' oppressors. Similarly, the Jews had no dealings with Samaritans. To understand what this story means in terms of inclusion, observe what Kenneth Davis has to say about a separate incident, that of the parable of the Good Samaritan.

> Samaritans did not have a great reputation among Jews. They were not good neighbors. The Jews and the Samaritans had a long and unhappy history. The Samaritans had first come into the land when the Assyrians conquered Israel. An offshoot sect, they followed the Books of Moses but did not treat the rest of the Hebrew Scriptures as sacred, and there was bad blood between the groups. To give some sense of how Jewish people then would have viewed a story with a Samaritan as the good guy, a modern equivalent might be called "The Good Palestinian Terrorist."[15]

From the Gentile woman to the Roman centurion, Jesus is genuinely pleased, perhaps even astounded, that great faith could be found outside the Chosen People. No doubt baseball fans, as well as owners and players, however belatedly, shared a similar experience when those outside the "white" lines were allowed to don hat and glove and play the game they loved.

Yet, despite Jesus' example of reaching out to Jews, Gentiles, Romans, and Samaritans alike, his apostles were not exactly quick studies. His early followers, including Peter, the Rock, the new leader of the fledgling faith community, had been preaching the Good News of the Lord only to the Jews. It wasn't until Peter had received a vision housed in a strange dream that he opened his mind to include Gentiles, much like centuries later when Eddie Stankey grew to accept Jackie Robinson.

"We are witnesses to all that he did both in Judea and in Jerusalem. They put him to death by hanging him on a tree; but God raised him on the third day and allowed him to appear, not to all the people but to us who were chosen by God as witnesses, and who ate and drank with him after he rose from the dead...."

While Peter was still speaking, the Holy Spirit fell upon all who heard the word. The circumcised believers who had come with Peter were astounded that the gift of the Holy Spirit had been poured out even on the Gentiles, for they heard them speaking in tongues and extolling God.

They praised God, saying, "Then God has given even to the Gentiles the repentance that leads to life" (Acts 10:39–41, 44–46; 11:18).

The Holy Spirit first descended upon the apostles and disciples on the feast of Pentecost. During this harvest festival, it was not unusual for people to travel to Jerusalem from places far and wide, including Arabia, Crete, Asia, even Rome. On this particular Pentecost, Peter and the apostles and others underwent a remarkable transformation.

When the day of Pentecost had come, they were all together in one place. And suddenly from heaven there came a sound like the rush of a violent wind, and it filled the entire house where they were sitting. Divided tongues, as of fire, appeared among them, and a tongue rested on each of them. All of them were filled with the Holy Spirit and began to speak in other languages, as the Spirit gave them ability.

Now there were devout Jews from every nation under heaven living in Jerusalem. And at this sound the crowd gathered and was bewildered, because each one heard them speaking in the native language of each. Amazed and astonished, they asked, "Are not all these who are speaking Galileans? And how is it that we hear, each of us, in our own native language? Parthians, Medes, Elamites, and residents of Mesopotamia, Judea and Cappadocia, Pontus and Asia, Phrygia and Pamphylia, Egypt and the parts of Libya belonging to Cyrene, and visitors from Rome, both Jews and proselytes, Cretans and Arabs—in our own languages we hear them speaking about God's deeds of power." All were amazed and perplexed, saying to one another, "What does this mean?" (Acts 2:1–12).

What does this mean, indeed?

Looking back, one might conclude that the word of God is meant to be heard by people of all nations. However, to paraphrase Luke in Acts one might reach a similar conclusion regarding our national pastime.

"Look, are not all these who play baseball? And how is it that we cheer, each in our own language those players from where we were born? Dominicans and Mexicans and Cubans, those dwelling in Venezuela, Puerto Rico and Panama, Korea and Japan, Australia and Columbia, China and the parts of Canada adjoining America, visitors and home teams, both whites and blacks, Latins and Asians, we see them playing our own game as a wonderful work of God."

Baseball, perhaps more than any other enterprise, brings together people of different religions, races, and nationalities, and forges them into thriving communities where all work together to serve one another toward a common goal.

Leave it to the game to hold out the possibility, the potential God sees for all of humanity.

Growing up, I was taught that Catholicism is the one true religion. These days at least the Church recognizes that there are many ways to the Father. Either way, the infant Church had to expand its thinking, go through a conversion of its own, to be inclusive of the much larger world of Gentiles. For its part, the national pastime had to mature before it could indeed reflect all that is good about America—inclusion, equality, freedom of expression. Christianity and baseball have long had ideals. It just took them both a while to live up to them.

"THE GIANTS WIN THE PENNANT! THE GIANTS WIN THE PENNANT!"1

The Miracle of Coogan's Bluff, October 3, 1951

"Which is easier, to say to the paralytic, 'Your sins are for-given,' or to say, 'Stand up and take your mat and walk'?"

MARK 2:9

WEBSTER DEFINES A "MIRACLE" as a wonder or marvel; an effect or extraordinary event in the physical world that surpasses all known human or natural powers and is ascribed to a supernatural cause; and such an effect or event manifesting or considered a work of God.2

For wonders or marvels, baseball offers examples of those nightly. One can view incredible plays in the field regularly during the "Web Gem" installment on ESPN's *Baseball Tonight.* Or for a compilation of marvelous mitt work, just take a look at a highlight reel of Hall of Fame shortstop Ozzie Smith. His acrobatic, gymnastic, fantastic plays in the field seemed to indicate that he knew where the ball would be before the ball did.

One play in particular stands out. As a San Diego Padre, Smith darted toward second base to field a hard hit ball up the middle. As he dove, stretching out to glove the grounder, the ball hit a rock or seam in the infield and bounced in the opposite direction. With what some might call a miraculous reaction, Ozzie reached back with his bare hand in mid-dive to snare the ball, hit belly first on the ground, bounced up, and threw a strike to first to nail the runner. And stun the baseball world. Is it any wonder, or marvel, that he was called the Wizard of Oz?

If an extraordinary event surpasses all known human powers, one can certainly ascribe it to a supernatural cause. The Big Bang that started it all would be a case in point. However, the Big Bang off the bat of St. Louis Cardinal slugger Mark McGwire that shattered Roger Maris' thirty-seven-year-old single season home run record of 61, while notable, would not be. For one, Big Mac went on to break his own record of 62 again and again to finish the season with a remarkable 70 round trippers, the first person in baseball history to reach that figure. For another, San Francisco Giant Barry Bonds broke that record just three seasons later by hitting 73. Both record-breaking instances underscore the key to this particular definition: human powers. One might argue that any baseball record set, however extraordinary, must be considered within the sphere of possibility, as all baseball players are human (with the possible exception of left-handed pitcher Bill "Spaceman" Lee, who was said to have been from another planet).

Now if one takes the position that a miracle is an impossible event that occurs once, never to be repeated again, then our national pastime has its fair share of miraculous events. Over his twenty-two-year career, pitcher Cy Young amassed a major league record 511 victories. He routinely started 46 games or more a season, completing an astounding 90 percent of them over the course of his career. He won more than 30 games a season on five separate occasions, and logged 7,356 innings overall (an average of 334 innings a year for 22 years!). In this day and age, starting pitchers rest four days between assignments, rarely make it through the seventh inning much less the ninth, and are considered workhorses if they average 35 starts and 250 innings a season. Chances are good that Cy Young's totals will never be surpassed, and therefore could be considered miraculous.

The same could be said for Nolan Ryan's seven no-hitters, Joe DiMaggio's 56-game hitting streak, Rickey Henderson's 1,400 plus stolen bases, and Cal Ripken's 2,632 consecutive game playing streak, Ty Cobb's lifetime batting average of .366, and Pete Rose's all-time hit total of 4,256. Of course, it should also be said that records are meant to be broken.

Our third definition of miracle is an effect or event manifesting or considered a work of God. These events fall roughly into two areas. The work of God, eternal and infinite, the supreme creator of all that is. And the work of God, the baseball fan.

Under the latter category would fall the seasons of the New York Giants of 1954, and the aptly named Miracle Mets of 1969. World Series winners both, yet not without—many say—a bit of divine intervention.

In 1954, the Cleveland Indians stood the baseball world on its ear. They finished ahead of a powerful Yankee club by eight games. And the Yankees won 103 games that year. The Tribe's 111 wins established a new league record. Their starting rotation of Bob Feller, Mike Garcia, Bob Lemon, and Early Wynn was considered one of the strongest in baseball history. Lemon and Wynn tied for the league lead in wins with 23; Garcia chipped in with 19 and led the league in earned run average at 2.64. The Indians were considered prohibitive favorites over the National League entry that year, the New York Giants.

Of course, all that was before "The Catch."

It is perhaps the most replayed fielding gem of all time. The ball hit into deep center field, the outfielder turning his back to the crowd, his number 24 racing to the deepest part of the ballpark, an over the shoulder catch, a whirling throw, his cap falling off. Of all the signature plays he made in his Hall of Fame career, for all the 660 home runs he hit, Willie Mays will be forever remembered for "The Catch."

Mays himself has said that he had made other catches that were far more difficult. But none were on the stage that is the World Series. It was the top of the eighth inning of the first game; the

Indians had two runners on base with no outs in a 2–2 tie. Tribe slugger Vic Wertz launched a tremendous blast to center field that would have cleared the fence were the game played in Cleveland instead of New York's Polo Grounds. Mays, seemingly at the point when ball and bat made contact, spun around, sprinted for a spot in deep center where only he and the baseball knew a meeting was scheduled.

The Catch prevented the Indians from scoring. The Catch deflated the Indians to such an extent that they were swept in four games. The Catch represented a miraculous start to a remarkable finish.

In 1969, events took place that players, sportswriters, and fans all over the country called miraculous. That season the Chicago Cubs, riding the talents of such stars as Ernie Banks, Ferguson Jenkins, Ron Santo, and Billy Williams, held a 9–1/2 game lead in early August. However, the New York Mets, punching bags and punch lines since coming into the league in 1962, went 38–11 in their last forty-nine games to roar past Chicago and leave the stunned Cubs eight games back when the dust had settled. Ward and Burns summarized the Met transformation: "In a single season the team that had been the laughingstock of the National League had become the Amazin' Mets."[3]

David Nemec and Saul Wisnia in their book, *Baseball: More Than 150 years*, use the "M" word in their recap of the 1969 season: "Mets Manager Gil Hodges was called a miracle worker...."[4] Newspapers all across the country were calling the club "The Miracle Mets." After New York swept the Braves three games to none in the first ever divisional championship series, who could blame them?

Going into the World Series, the Mets were decided underdogs against the American League champion Baltimore Orioles. The Birds led their league in pitching, won 109 games in the regular season, and swept the Minnesota Twins in the league championship series. The fact that the Orioles limited the Mets to just four hits in their opening game victory only further exposed the mismatch.

But New York still had a miracle or two up their Met blue sleeves. A young reliever named Nolan Ryan (yes, that Nolan Ryan) chipped in to help shut out the Orioles in game two. Center fielder Tommy Agee and right fielder Ron Swoboda made spectacular catches to preserve wins. Platoon player Donn Clendenon hit three home runs in four games. And Al Weis, a lifetime .219 hitter, batted .455. The result? Four wins in a row to capture their first World Series title.

Ward and Burns put it in perspective: "The unthinkable had happened. An American had stepped on the moon earlier that summer and for New Yorkers it was hard to say which was the greater miracle."5

Yet these examples, while incredible in their own right, pale in comparison to the Miracle of Coogan's Bluff. Set on baseball's grandest stage, New York City, this one had all of the nail-biting, eye-closing, prayer-inducing, jaw-dropping, and heart-pounding drama anyone could ask for, baseball fan or not.

On August 12, 1951, the New York Giants found themselves 13–1/2 games behind their bitter rivals, the Brooklyn Dodgers. In one of the most exciting finishes in major league history, the Giants took 39 of their last 47 games, including 16 in a row in August. The Dodgers, on the other hand, needed 14 innings on the last day of the season to defeat the Phillies to force a three-game playoff.

The two teams split the first two games, with the Giants winning the opener, 3–1, while "da bums" avoided elimination in game two with a 10–0 shutout, courtesy of rookie Clem Labine (whose name adorned the first baseball glove I ever owned). Everything came down to the winner-take-all third game.

Riding the tired arm of ace Don Newcombe as far as they could, Brooklyn held a 4–1 lead with one out in the bottom of the ninth. However, Newk had given everything he had, so much so that his last pitch was hit for a double by Whitey Lockman. The Giants had cut the lead to 4–2, and now had runners on second and third. His bullpen depleted, Brooklyn manager Charlie Dressen brought in starting pitcher Ralph Branca to face Bobby Thomson, who had hit 31 home runs during the year. On Branca's second pitch, Thomson swung and, well, here's how Giants play-by-play announcer, Russ Hodges, described it:

> Branca throws…There's a long drive…It's gonna be…I believe!…The Giants win the pennant! The Giants win the pennant! The Giants win the pennant! The Giants win the pennant! Bobby Thomson hits into the lower deck of the left field stands. The Giants win the pennant and they're going crazy! Ohhhhh! I don't believe it! I don't believe it! I don't believe it![6]

A miracle? For some "the shot heard 'round the world" had gone beyond that. Ward and Burns recall one particularly incredulous commentary by one of American's most renowned sportswriters:

> "The art of fiction is dead," wrote Red Smith. "Reality has strangled invention. Only the utterly impossible, the inexpressibly fantastic, can ever be plausible again."[7]

If Willie Mays' fielding heroics in the 1954 World Series is the most shown catch of all time, Bobby Thomson's dramatic home run against the Dodgers in 1951 is quite possibly the most viewed hit. Indeed, the Giants had won the National League pennant in what the baseball world calls the Miracle of Coogan's Bluff.

Yet as amazing as these events were, and to some they have been considered miraculous, they all were of human hands. Talented, driven, inspired, and fortunate hands, but human nonetheless. As to whether or not God the baseball fan worked through these hands, only those players who came out of, and returned to, the Iowa cornfields in the movie *Field of Dreams* can say.

A true miracle is heaven sent, by God through the Spirit. A miracle is a message from on high that there is an awe-inducing power greater than baseball—even a force of goodness and love—that calls us to those very same qualities that reside deep within us.

Just as players pass the traditions of the game down from generation to generation, teaching us to value the history and art that is our national pastime, so too do we have an ancestor who has shown us the way to God. Jesus Christ, the Son of God, the second Person of the Blessed Trinity, walked our earth some two thousand years ago, preaching and teaching us a better way to play the game of life.

And just as baseball has its evangelists, such as Roger Angell, Ken Burns, David Halberstam, and Roger Kahn, to chronicle the game's exploits and tout its virtues, so too did Matthew, Mark, Luke, and John record the "good news" that was and still is Christ.

In order that we might believe that he was both God and man, paradoxically 100 percent divine and 100 percent human, Jesus performed signs throughout his ministry to authenticate his mission. In the Gospel of John, the author records seven such signs (seven being the biblical number of plenty). Each of these miracles helped show Christ's divinity and substantiate his being the Messiah.

Through his works, however, Jesus was both accepted and rejected. There were some Jews and Gentiles who truly believed that Jesus was the Messiah in their midst. There were considerably more who were expecting a political or military savior to rescue them from Roman persecution. The religious leaders of the day, feeling their own sense of power threatened, did not help matters any by denouncing Jesus as a heretic.

John recorded the first miracle of Jesus' ministry, that of turning water into wine at the wedding feast of Cana. By doing so, Jesus revealed his power over nature. That water and wine were featured is also quite significant. When Jesus met the Samaritan woman at the well, he said to her: "*Everyone who drinks of this water will be thirsty again, but those who drink of the water that I will give them will never be thirsty. The water that I will give will become in them a spring of water gushing up to eternal life"* (John 4:13–14).

Later in John's Gospel, during the Jewish Feast of the Tabernacles where an intricate water ritual takes place, Christ cried out saying, *"Let anyone who is thirsty come to me, and let the one who believes in me drink. As the scripture has said, 'Out of the believer's heart shall flow rivers of living water'"* (John 7:37–38).

Wine plays an integral part in the Catholic Mass, where during the consecration, the Church community re-creates Christ's Last Supper. At that meal, Jesus instituted the sacrament of the Eucharist, where his apostles and now we share, through bread and wine, in his body and blood. *Then he took a cup, and after giving thanks he gave it to them, saying, "Drink from it, all of you; for this is my blood of the covenant, which is poured out for many for the forgiveness of sins"* (Matthew 26:27–28). In so doing, Jesus eclipsed the covenant God had made with the Jews through Abraham.

Finally, as Jesus lay dead on the cross…*one of the soldiers pierced his side with a spear, and at once blood and water came out* (John 19:34). Blood transformed from wine, the living water. The water and wine from the wedding feast at Cana comes full circle.

With the curing of a nobleman's son, Jesus performed his second sign. In this case, Jesus not only showed that he had power over sickness, but could transcend space. He need not be present to physically cure the child. What's more, by curing the son of a nobleman, in effect a servant of the governing powers, the Romans, Christ was not limiting his kingdom to a certain social or economic class. Anyone who believed in him, and he who sent him, was welcome. Finally, belief without seeing is an integral part of Christian, and baseball, faith. Just ask any fan who has ever prayed for a walk-off home run in the bottom of the ninth inning while listening to their home team on the radio.

With the words *"Stand up and take your mat and walk,"* Christ performed his third miracle, the healing of a man who had been crippled for thirty-eight years. With this sign, Jesus fulfilled a prophesy of Isaiah who had predicted that the Messiah would cure the lame: *The lame shall leap like a deer* (Isaiah 35:6). However, Christ had angered the religious leaders by performing a miracle on the Sabbath, a day when all devout Jews were to worship, not work. Jesus maintained that he could do nothing without God's blessing. In effect, he was saying, if it's OK by the Father to cure on the Sabbath, it's OK by me. Jesus demonstrated the human trait of compassion for the infirm man, and divinity by revealing an equal relationship with God the Father. Christ also asked a question of the afflicted man that we might do well to consider: "Do you want to be made well?"

One might expect Jesus to shake up the establishment by righting a wrong and pursuing the greater good. After all, he is equal parts divine and human. But there have been mere humans who have done the same, on the fields of play no less. In 1947, Branch Rickey, general manager of the Brooklyn Dodgers, forever changed the game and advanced the cause of civil rights long before our government did. By signing Jackie Robinson, an African-American, to play for his club, Rickey brought the ire of the league, fans, the press, opponents, and even members of his own team upon Robinson and himself. When Robinson signed with Montreal, the Dodgers' AAA farm team, the organization said, "We made this step for two reasons. First, we are signing this boy because we think of him primarily as a ballplayer. Second, we think it is a point of fairness."[8] By recognizing Robinson's talents as a baseball player and a person, the Dodgers opened the door for equality in baseball.

Jesus himself said: *"I am the vine, you are the branches. Those who abide in me and I in them bear much fruit..."* (John 15:5). Thanks to this particular Branch, the game of baseball in particular and society in general has been very blessed.

Batting cleanup in the miracle lineup was the famous transformation of the loaves and the fishes, an event that had a tremendous impact on those present. To recap, Jesus transformed five barley loaves and two fish into food to feed more than five thousand people with enough left over to fill twelve baskets.

Jesus' humanity is shown by the fact that, like his followers, he was dependent upon food. He appreciated the fellowship of his disciples. And was aware of the great need of the multitude. By the miracle of the loaves and fishes, Christ demonstrated his divinity, and equality with God the Creator, by creating more from less. Not only that, but the gathering of the twelve baskets symbolically suggested that there would be food for the soul for the twelve apostles as well as the twelve tribes of Israel. As with the wine at Cana, the blessing of the bread and giving thanks foreshadowed the breaking of the bread at the Last Supper. Lastly, a lesson can be learned from the young boy who shared the original five loaves and two fishes. By sharing what we have with others, we in effect extend, or multiply, the love God has for us. By making a conscious, intentional effort, we too can make great things happen.

That same evening, Jesus performed his fifth sign: walking on water and calming the storm. Though Jesus had already shown his mastery over nature, he still felt the need to perform signs so that the masses might come to believe that he was truly the Son of God, for only through his Father was he able to perform such miracles. To be able to command the wind and the sea, not to mention walk on water or instantly transport a boat, was further proof to his disciples of his messianic mission. Taking a look at this account in Mark's Gospel sheds further light on this particular sign.

And they were utterly astounded, for they did not understand about the loaves, but their hearts were hardened (6:51–52).

No wonder Jesus had to perform sign after sign, miracle after miracle. Even his handpicked followers, his posse, if you will, had trouble grasping the magnitude of it all. Their hearts were hardened; they were fearful of what they were experiencing. Thus Christ's words to console them, to uplift them. How often might we be consoled or uplifted if we were to soften our hearts? As Mark relates, *"Take heart, it is I; do not be afraid"* (6:50).

With the curing of a blind man, the Lord's sixth sign again fulfilled a prophecy of Isaiah, *"The eyes of the blind shall be opened"* (35:5). It was yet another example of the works Jesus told to John the Baptist. *"Go and tell John what you hear and see: the blind receive their sight, the lame walk, the lepers are cleansed, the deaf hear, the dead are raised, and the poor have good news brought to them"* (Matthew 11:4–5). Talk about your lineup of miracles.

The last of John's seven recorded signs is by far the most dramatic and impressive—the raising of Lazarus from the dead.

When Jesus arrived, he found that Lazarus had already been in the tomb four days....When Martha heard that Jesus was coming, she went and met him, while Mary stayed at home. Martha said to Jesus, "Lord, if you had been here, my brother would not have died. But even now I know that God will give you whatever you ask of him...."

Then Jesus, again greatly disturbed, came to the tomb. It was a cave, and a stone was lying against it. Jesus said, "Take away the stone." Martha, the sister of the dead man, said to him, "Lord, already there is a stench because he has been dead four days." Jesus said to her, "Did I not tell you that if you believed, you would see the glory of God?" So they took away the stone. And Jesus looked upward and said, "Father, I thank you for having heard me. I knew that you always hear me, but I have said this for the sake of the crowd standing here, so that they may believe that you sent me." When he had said this, he cried with a loud voice, "Lazarus, come out!" The dead man came out, his hands and feet bound with strips of cloth, and his face wrapped in a cloth. Jesus said to them, "Unbind him, and let him go" (John 11:17, 20–22, 38–44).

Talk about marvels and wonders. Here Jesus accomplished the unfathomable—raising a man from the dead. In so doing, Christ revealed heartfelt emotion. He was so overcome he groaned. John says, *Jesus began to weep. So the Jews said, "See how he loved him!"* (John 11:35). They may have tears of grief that Christ wept for his friend and his sisters. They may have been tears of sadness that, as a human, Lazarus would have to face death again. Perhaps Jesus was anticipating his own death. Or the fact that it had come to this, after all the words he had preached and works he had performed, there were still those with him who doubted his ministry.

Regardless, as he had done time and again, Jesus called upon the love of his Father and performed the miracle of miracles. True, modern medicine has allowed doctors to resuscitate victims who have been technically dead in that their hearts had stopped. But Lazarus had been pronounced dead, wrapped in grave clothes, and been entombed for four days! Jesus had demonstrated power over nature, the elements, sickness, handicaps, and now death itself. The stage was set for his own death—and overcoming it by his resurrection.

In the couplet that began this inning, Jesus asked which was easier, to forgive a paralytic of his sins or to say arise and walk? Similarly, if we have doubts of faith, if we question whether Jesus walked on water or turned water into wine, perhaps we should consider baseball. After all, if the Miracle Mets can win the World Series in 1969, and if the 1951 Giants can be the willing recipients of the Miracle of Coogan's Bluff, who's to say that miracles can't happen?

Bill DeWitt Jr., current St. Louis Cardinals owner, gets a hitting lesson from the Babe, George Herman Ruth.

The late broadcaster
Lindsey Nelson cel-
ebrates with the
"Ol' Perfessor,"
Casey Stengel.

"Déjà vu all over again,"
Yogi Berra.

All-time lefty winner, pitcher Warren Spahn.

Home run king Hank Aaron is interviewed by broadcasting legend Harry Caray.

Dodger great Jackie Robinson leaps for a double play throw after forcing out Cardinals second baseman Red Schoendienst.

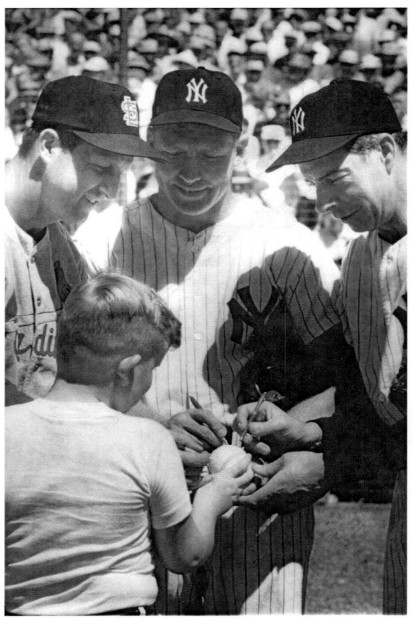

Baseball legends Stan Musial, Mickey Mantle, and Joe DiMaggio sign autographs before a spring training game in 1961.

Hall of Famer Sandy Koufax
in his classic wind-up.

Boston Red Sox
star Ted Williams,
the Splendid
Splinter.

Top: Nolan Ryan going for another strikeout.
Bottom: Five-tool player Willie Mays drives one into left.

Bob "Gibby" Gibson "intimidates" Cubs third baseman Ron Santo.

"755 Career Home Runs; 11 Career Home Runs"

This is the record of Aaron and Moses

This is the lineage of Aaron and Moses.

NUMBERS 3:1

NUMBERS IS THE FOURTH BOOK OF THE BIBLE and of the Torah. Numbers are also what the game of baseball is built on. A team's success or failure depends upon the number of wins or losses in a season. A player's salary reflects the kind of numbers he puts up and, if not his ranking on the team, then the shrewdness of his agent. A franchise's profitability is partly dictated by the number of fans in the stands; its success by the number of pennants that fly over its stadium. There are even cottage industries devoted to numbers: the Elias Sports Bureau provides any kind of baseball statistic you can imagine, such as how many home runs Alex Rodriguez has hit against the Indians in day games following Yankee victories the previous night celebrated by guacamole and chips after the games. Well, not quite that arcane. Bill James has made a career out of his *Baseball Abstract*, which takes statistics of players and evaluates them by isolating particular variables, such as night games, or men in scoring position, to give a clearer picture of a player's relative value to his team in comparison to his peers. In 2002, the Red Sox even hired James as a senior advisor.

In the biblical version of Numbers, Moses and his brother Aaron are in the midst of leading the Jewish people to the Promised Land. That's one way to put it. Another is to say that the brothers are still wandering in the wilderness. In the book, we learn of manna in the desert, conversations between God and Moses, the people rebelling against the leadership of Moses, and the actual borders of the Promised Land. And showing that ballplayers aren't the only ones who make mental errors, we read about Moses misinterpreting God's instructions.

Moses is one of the key figures in the Old Testament; his story is one of the most well known of the Bible. In Exodus, we read how as an infant he escaped the blanket death sentence of all Jewish boys by order of the Egyptian Pharaoh. His mother placed him in a basket made of reeds to let her son set sail unaccompanied down the Nile, the river that is an essential source of all life in Egypt. Eventually, the baby in a basket was found by Pharaoh's daughter, taken in, and given the name Moses (Egyptian for "son of").

Raised in the royal court, Moses was in effect treated as a "son of" the Pharaoh. Things took a turn for the historic when Moses witnessed the brutal beating of a Hebrew worker by that man's Egyptian superior. In attempting to intervene, Moses killed the overseer, then fled the scene of the crime to the land of Midian, where he married, had a family and settled down to the life of a shepherd.

God had other plans. In the well-known story of the burning bush, God spoke to Moses and appointed him savior of the Jews, telling him that he must return to Egypt to lead his people out of slavery into the Promised Land. Along the way ten plagues fell upon Egypt, the waters of the Red Sea were parted, and Moses received the Ten Commandments from atop Mount Sinai.

However, as the story of Numbers is recounted, the Jewish people were quite upset that here they were wandering the desert with no food or water. Then Moses did what so many ballplayers have done at one time or another in their careers—he missed a sign.

"Why have you brought us up out of Egypt, to bring us to this wretched place? It is no place for grain, or figs, or vines, or pomegranates; and there is no water to drink." Then Moses and Aaron went away from the assembly to the entrance of the tent of meeting; they fell on their faces, and the glory of the LORD appeared to them.

The LORD spoke to Moses, saying: Take the staff, and assemble the congregation, you and your brother Aaron, and command the rock before their eyes to yield its water. Thus you shall bring water out of the rock for them; thus you shall provide drink for the congregation....

Moses and Aaron gathered the assembly together before the rock, and he said to them, "Listen, you rebels, shall we bring water for you out of this rock?" Then Moses lifted up his hand and struck the rock twice with his staff; water came out abundantly, and the congregation and their livestock drank (Numbers 20:5–8, 10–11).

Moses struck the rock twice with his staff. However, God did not give Moses the "sign" to swing away. By instructing Moses to "speak to the rock" instead of striking it, God in effect gave Moses the take sign. As usually happens when a player misses a sign, there were repercussions.

"Because you did not trust in me, to show my holiness before the eyes of the Israelites, therefore you shall not bring this assembly into the land that I have given them" (Numbers 20:12).

Despite his special relationship with God, Moses was denied entrance to the Promised Land. And he wasn't the only Moses to miss out.

Jerry and John Moses (he of the 11 career home runs) played in the major leagues a combined twenty years, for a total of nine different teams. Their wandering in the baseball desert took them to Anaheim, Boston, Chicago, Cleveland, Detroit, Minnesota, New

York, San Diego, and Seattle. Never once did they reach the Promised Land of a world championship.

Wally Moses played seventeen years for the Philadelphia A's, Chicago White Sox, and Boston Red Sox. In all that time he only went to the World Series once in 1946 as a member of the Red Sox. Though he hit .417 in four games, his Boston team fell to the St. Louis Cardinals, four games to three. Even a Moses could not overcome the Curse of the Bambino.

Biblical Moses has taught us that though we may have a special relationship with God, that God loves us unequivocally, our lives, our dreams, our wishes may turn out differently than we had hoped. Moses is one of the few people in the history of humankind that we know of to have actually conversed with God. The Almighty gave Moses the Ten Commandments. Moses was the one selected to lead the Chosen People out of captivity from Egypt. God even allowed Moses to be in his presence, though Moses had to turn his face so as not to be overcome by the brilliance that is God. Despite all this, Moses was denied his place in the Promised Land.

Baseball's Ernie Banks suffered much the same fate.

The man known as Mr. Cub was blessed with strong wrists, strong legs, and a love for the game. Though slim at 6'1" and 180 pounds, he had the power to hit the ball all around the park and over the wall. In his nineteen years as a beloved Chicago Cub, Banks hit 512 home runs, drove in 1,636 runs, and won back-to-back Most Valuable Player Awards in 1958–1959, becoming the first player in baseball history to earn the honor while playing for a losing team. He led the league in home runs and RBIs twice, and played in ten All-Star games. Equally adept in the field, he earned a Gold Glove at shortstop, leading the league in fielding three times. After moving to first base in 1962 due to an ailing knee, he garnered more put outs than any other National League first sacker five times.

Yet for all this, he never once played in the World Series.

Though disappointed at not having a chance to play on baseball's grand stage, Banks realized how fortunate, how blessed he was to be given the gifts to play a game he loved. He is fondly remembered as much for his playing as for his oft-repeated phrase that captured the affection he and most players have for the game: "What a great day for baseball. Let's play two!"[1]

From the banks of the Nile to the Banks of Wrigley Field, Moses and Ernie teach us that our journeys may not take us to the place of our dreams. But there is much to be gained from following the will of God and the love of the game.

As we saw in Numbers 20:12, Aaron, too, was denied access to the Promised Land. However, that's not to say he didn't find favor with God.

The LORD spoke to Moses, saying: Speak to Aaron and his sons, saying, Thus you shall bless the Israelites: You shall say to them,
The LORD bless you and keep you;
the LORD make his face to shine upon you,
and be gracious to you;
the LORD lift up his countenance upon you,
and give you peace (Numbers 6:22–26).

This Aaronic benediction as it's called is one of the most precious of all blessings, and is still used today as an example of God's love for his people. It also was quite prophetic in terms of the game of baseball. While Aaron of the Bible may not have reached the Promised Land, Aaron of the ball field did. And was blessed in doing so.

[Behold] the staff of Aaron (Numbers 17:8).

To eliminate the continued complaints of the Israelites as to Moses' and Aaron's divine instruction, each of the twelve families was instructed to give Moses a staff. The staff that budded would indicate from which family the tribes' leadership would come. From these twelve dead sticks, the staff of Aaron, from the House of Levi, budded, giving forth blossoms and ripe almonds no less.

And, behold, the bat of Aaron.

Milwaukee and Atlanta Brave Hank Aaron reached two promised lands, and it's difficult to say which proved to be the most cherished trip. As a young twenty-three-year-old right fielder, Aaron was a member of the Milwaukee teams that won back-to-back National League pennants in 1957 and 1958. Aaron and third baseman Eddie Mathews supplied the power; Warren Spahn and Lew Burdette provided the pitching to propel the Braves into two fall classic confrontations with the New York Yankees. Each Series went the maximum seven games; each team was able to claim for itself a world title, with the Braves taking the honor in 1957. In twenty-three years of playing major league baseball, that was the only time Aaron could call himself champion. But it was not the only time he would find himself in first place.

Aaron ventured into another promised land much later in his career, this time alone. He entered a land of giants (and Red Sox and Twins and Athletics) and slew them one by one, overtaking such paragons of power as Mel Ott, Eddie Mathews, Ted Williams, Harmon Killebrew, Jimmie Foxx, and Willie Mays. All in pursuit of the legendary Babe Ruth and his all-time home run record of 714. Ruth's record wasn't the only thing that Aaron had to overcome. During his career and his drive for the record, baseball's ugly face of prejudice rose up again.

From Gerald Astor's book comes this recollection of Aaron's teammate and former manager Eddie Mathews, "...with Aaron, there were times when he wasn't even allowed in the dining car of the train. We'd have to bring his meal back to him."[2]

"What is Aaron that you rail against him?" (Numbers 16:11).

In the Bible, Aaron had the difficulty of being Moses' brother. There was much jealousy at the brothers' special relationship with God. In baseball, Aaron, despite his gifts, endured the difficulties of being black. Both men had to draw upon an inner strength to help see them through adversity. For Aaron in the desert, it was a faith in his God-given instructions; for Aaron in the ballpark it was a faith in his God-given talent. To get an idea of some of what the latter day Aaron had to face, let's turn to Ward and Burns:

Dear Nigger: You black animal, I hope you never live long enough to hit more home runs than the great Babe Ruth.

Dear Hank Aaron: I hope you get it between the eyes.

Dear Nigger Henry: It has come to my attention that you are going to break Babe Ruth's record....I will be going to the rest of your games and if you hit one more home run it will be your last. My gun will be watching your every black move....3

Undeterred, Aaron kept on hammering home runs. He hit 40 during the 1973 season to arrive at 713. Then the following spring, on April 8, 1974, he took an Al Downing fast ball to deep left field in Dodger Stadium to finally pass the Sultan of Swat and become the new king of the long ball.

In his career, baseball's Aaron won the National League Most Valuable Player once, led the league in batting twice, home runs four times (including a tie), doubles four times, and RBI four times. He was selected to 21 All-Star teams; he even stole 240 bases. For his career he hit 755 home runs and drove in 2,297 runs, tops in both categories. Four times he hit 44 home runs, the same number that adorned his back. But as so often happens with numbers, they only tell part of the story.

For the Israelites to reach the Promised Land, they had to wander in the desert for forty years. For Hank Aaron, he had to endure years of bigotry. It is said that God does not give us more than we can handle. Hank Aaron won the respect of all of baseball that day in April when he hit number 715. He won the admiration of a country, though he had won the love of African Americans years before.

So Moses struck the rock twice and anyone named Moses struck out in their attempt at a world championship. Brother Aaron did not swing at the rock and Hank Aaron etched his name in the record books. A case of biblical cause and baseball effect? Hardly. If that were the case, we'd also be reading about the exploits of Hank's brother, Tommie. As it was, Tommie's seven-year career statistics amount to a single mediocre season for his famous sibling.

We all have our respective paths to travel. Some of us will make it to our desired destinations, whether the Promised Land, World Series, chairman of the board, or parent. Some of us will come up short. But all of us have a part to play in God's mysterious master plan and should, as Ernie Banks has taught us, make the most of our journey along the way. Without these men named Moses and Aaron, and their respective contributions large and small, the Bible and the game would not be what they are today. The same can be said about each one of us and the world in which we live.

"HIT, HIT WITH POWER, RUN, FIELD, AND THROW"

Classic definition of the five-tool player

"To the one he gave five talents...."

MATTHEW 25:15

TAKE IN ANY MAJOR LEAGUE BASEBALL GAME. You'll be amazed at the talent on the field. You'll see hard-throwing right handers and slick fielding shortstops, wall-scaling outfielders and prodigious batsmen. If the ballplayers were to look in the stands, they'd too see a vast array of gifted people. Fans at night, they might be surgeons, mechanics, lawyers, musicians, chefs, or artists during the day. Each of us has God-given talents. Our task is to make the most of them. For lessons in how to do just this, one need only look as far as the Bible and baseball.

Jesus often used parables to teach his followers—Aesop's Fables of a sort with a spiritual lesson attached. This was in part because his message was so contrary to teachings of the time that he had to couch it terms that were more palatable to the masses and religious leaders alike. And what could be more palatable than what was in effect a children's bedtime story for an older audience. One such tale told of nurturing our talents.

"For it is as if a man, going on a journey, summoned his slaves and entrusted his property to them; to one he gave five talents, to another two, to another one, to each according to his ability. Then

he went away. The one who had received the five talents went off at once and traded with them, and made five more talents. In the same way, the one who had the two talents made two more talents. But the one who had received the one talent went off and dug a hole in the ground and hid his master's money. After a long time the master of those slaves came and settled accounts with them. Then the one who had received the five talents came forward, bringing five more talents, saying, 'Master, you handed over to me five talents; see, I have made five more talents.' His master said to him, 'Well done, good and trustworthy slave; you have been trustworthy in a few things, I will put you in charge of many things; enter into the joy of your master.' And the one with the two talents also came forward, saying, 'Master, you handed over to me two talents; see, I have made two more talents.' His master said to him, 'Well done, good and trustworthy slave; you have been trustworthy in a few things, I will put you in charge of many things; enter into the joy of your master.' Then the one who had received the one talent also came forward, saying, 'Master, I knew that you were a harsh man, reaping where you did not sow, and gathering where you did not scatter seed; so I was afraid, and I went and hid your talent in the ground. Here you have what is yours.' But his master replied, 'You wicked and lazy slave! You knew, did you, that I reap where I did not sow, and gather where I did not scatter? Then you ought to have invested my money with the bankers, and on my return I would have received what was my own with interest. So take the talent from him, and give it to the one with the ten talents. For to all those who have, more will be given, and they will have an abundance; but from those who have nothing, even what they have will be taken away. As for this worthless slave, throw him into the outer darkness, where there will be weeping and gnashing of teeth'" (Matthew 25:14–30).

Jesus spoke of monetary units as a metaphor for God-given talents. Baseball people also speak of talents. Not surprisingly, they, too, place a significant emphasis on five talents: a player's ability to hit for average, hit for power, run, field, and throw. When these same folks talk of trades (as in the lopsided variety), one that immediately comes to mind is the Cincinnati Reds' exchange of right fielder Frank Robinson for pitcher Milt Pappas of the Baltimore Orioles and two other, lesser known players.

Frank Robinson could hit for average (he had nine seasons of a .300 mark or better), hit for power (as his 586 lifetime home runs attest), run (few people realize that Robinson stole over 200 bases in his career), field and throw (he was also a Gold Glove outfielder). In 1961, he led the Reds to their first World Series in twenty-one years, winning the National League Most Valuable Player award along the way. In his ten years with the team, Robinson *averaged* .303 in batting with 32 home runs and 100 RBIs. However, general manager Bill DeWitt felt Robinson's skills were on the decline and so unloaded the "fading" star to the Orioles.

"The one who had received the five talents went off at once and traded with them, and made five more talents." The six-time National League All-Star took with him his five talents, and made another five. In 1966, his first year with Baltimore, Robinson did nothing more than lead the league in batting average, home runs, and RBIs (.316/49/122), winning the Most Valuable Player Award to go with this Triple Crown. What's more, the Orioles flew right past Los Angeles in the World Series, sweeping the Dodgers in four games, with (you guessed it) Robinson being selected MVP of the Series as well. Not content to rest on his laurels, Robinson helped lead the O's to three more American League pennants as well as a victory in the 1970 fall classic. He was also named an American League All-Star five times and later elected to the baseball Hall of Fame. "Here's to you, Mr. Robinson," for taking your five talents from Cincinnati and reaping reward after reward with your new team in Baltimore. As for us, in whatever our situation, we owe it to ourselves and others to make the best use of our talents, our gifts from the Father.

Sometimes it takes awhile before we discover our own talents or, once discovered, for them to blossom. Perhaps we need the tutelage of a mentor, the encouragement of parent or teacher. Maybe a change of scenery is all it takes, a new job, a new relationship, a new place to live. In baseball, sometimes it takes a trade, another team having faith in a player, for their talents to shine.

In 1964, as they struggled to remain in the pennant race, the St. Louis Cardinals traded a former 20-game winner, Ernie Broglio, to the Chicago Cubs for an undistinguished outfielder named Lou Brock. In his book *October 1964*, David Halberstam described the new Card in the St. Louis deck:

Brock was twenty-four years old at the time, and he was not a particularly good outfielder, he had not hit very well in his brief time in the major leagues, and he had an erratic arm. Worse, after two full seasons, he was nothing more than a .260 hitter. An outfielder who was a defensive liability and who hit only .250 or .260 was not exactly a gem.[1]

However, what Brock could do was run... and run and run. His speed was likened to that of Cool Papa Bell. Given the freedom to steal bases, Brock rocked. He hit .348 for the Cardinals and stole 33 bases in his time with the team that year. As a mainstay of the Cardinals for more than fourteen seasons, sweet Lou, as he was nicknamed, helped St. Louis claim three National League pennants and two World Series titles, including the one in 1964.

Speed, of course, does not do you much good sitting on the bench. Given the chance, Brock showcased his talent to hit *and* run. He batted over .300 eight times, finishing his career with a lifetime .293 average, accumulating 3,023 hits in the process. Though the eighth commandment states *"You shall not steal"* (Exodus 20:15), baseball has earned a special dispensation. So it was that Brock led the league in stolen bases eight times, setting a then single season mark for thefts with 118 in 1974. His larcenous behavior as well as his talent for getting on base was rewarded with election to the Hall of Fame in 1985.

There are those whose talents have shown and grown as lilies of the baseball field. Pete Rose stretched his talents enough to make the National League All-Star team sixteen times at five—count them five—different positions: first, second, and third bases, and left and right fields. The National League MVP in 1973, he was a member of Cincinnati's Big Red Machine. Along with Joe Morgan, Johnny Bench, and Tony Perez, Rose brought back-to-back world titles to the Queen City in 1975 and 1976. He also was an integral part of the 1980 Philadelphia Phillie team that at long last gave a world championship to the City of Brotherly Love, the team's first title in ninety-eight years. And with 4,256, Rose collected more hits than anyone who ever played.

But one could say that the Hit King also buried his talent. A penchant for gambling and his subsequent banishment from baseball for allegedly betting on the game has kept this Rose from decorating baseball's Hall of Fame. At one point during his career, Ward and Burns report, Rose said,

> Baseball is a hard game. Love it hard and it will love you back hard. Try to play it easy and ease off and the first thing you know, there you are, on the outside, looking in, wondering what went wrong.[2]

It seems biblical prophets are not the only ones with insights to the future. Pete Rose is on the outside, looking in, and no doubt wondering what went wrong.

Even players with a single dominating talent have learned to nurture their gift to help it grow. Three of the greatest pitchers to ever toe the rubber had very similar beginnings, all inauspicious. Sandy Koufax, Nolan Ryan, and Randy Johnson posted a combined won-lost record of 152–150 in their first five seasons. During those fifteen years, the three fireballers notched winning records a grand total of five times. It took catcher Norm Sherry suggesting to Koufax that he didn't need to throw so hard to be effective to turn the left-hander's career around. For Ryan, the turning point came when his talents were traded to, perhaps not coincidentally, the Angels. As for Johnson, he credits conversations with Ryan as being instrumental in his learning how to pitch.

Separately, the three have compiled more than 700 victories and 12,000 strikeouts and still counting (for Johnson). Ryan and Koufax combined for 11 no-hitters, with Nolan throwing 7 of the no-nos, and Sandy pitching a perfect game. In 2004, the Big Unit tossed his own perfecto. Koufax and Johnson have won eight Cy Young Awards as outstanding pitcher in their leagues. All three have played on world champion teams, all three will call Cooperstown home.

Roger Clemens and Dennis Eckersley were two other pitchers who turned their singular talents into something more. Clemens, a hard-throwing Texan like Ryan, incorporated a fork ball into his pitching repertoire late in his career as he charged toward 300 wins and 4,000 strikeouts. Along the way, Clemens won seven Cy Youngs while pitching for four different teams and helped the Yankees to a pair of World Series titles in 1999 and 2000. For his part, Eckersley transformed himself from a starting pitcher with a twenty-game win-ning season and no-hitter to his credit to the most dominating relief pitcher of his era. Eck won close to 200 games and saved another 390 in his 20-plus seasons, earning his own Cy Young along the way, as well as a World Series ring with the 1989 A's and induction into the Hall of Fame.

Though it may seem fixed and stagnant, the Catholic religion is always moving, changing, evolving. However, it moves to its own clock and, given that God is timeless, maybe to no clock at all. This might explain why it took more than three centuries for the Church to reverse its stance on Galileo being a heretic for some of his early scientific observations. During my lifetime though, I've actually seen changes within the Church. The practice of never having meat on any Friday to commemorate Christ's dying on the cross was replaced with no meat on Fridays during Lent. Masses celebrated in Latin with the priest's back to the congregation evolved into Masses performed in a country's native tongue by priests facing the people. Today, celebration of the Eucharist allows participants to take both the consecrated bread and wine. Similarly, people's attitudes toward faith also change and evolve. As youngsters, we may focus more on strict adherence to right and wrong and the following of rules. As we grow older, our faith may mature to reflect service to, and tolerance of, others.

"I was afraid, and I went and hid your talent in the ground." For as many stories of tribulation and triumph, baseball also has its tales of talents wasted and opportunities lost. In 1962 a rookie pitcher burst upon the scene for the expansion Los Angeles Angels. Bo Belinsky won ten games for the halos, including a no-hitter. An instant celebrity for the first-year franchise, Bo played the beau around town, being seen at trendy Los Angeles night spots escorting starlets such as Mamie Van Doren. Unfortunately, he paid more attention to partying than pitching. He never lived up to the promise of his first campaign, winning only eighteen games in the next seven years, playing for four different teams in his last four seasons.

Mentioned in an earlier chapter, one of the greatest hitters to ever play the game forfeited the right to pursue his passion. Shoeless Joe Jackson, with a .356 lifetime batting average, was forced out of the game he loved for his connection with Black Sox scandal during the 1919 World Series. So great was his loss that he played outlaw baseball on several teams in the south under assumed names. Ward and Burns capture Jackson's regret:

[Shoeless Joe had] opened up a liquor store in Greenville, South Carolina. Ty Cobb once came in for a fifth of bourbon. Jackson did not seem to recognize his old rival. Cobb finally asked, "Don't you know me, Joe?"

"Sure—I know you, Ty," Jackson answered. "I just didn't think anyone I used to know up there wanted to recognize *me* again."[3]

Jose Canseco was a former teammate of Dennis Eckersley on the powerhouse Oakland A's of 1988–1990. Those teams went to three World Series in a row, winning the championship in 1989 with a 4–0 sweep of the Giants during the earthquake games. At the time, Canseco was one of the most feared sluggers in baseball, winning two home run titles and an MVP award. Together with Mark McGwire they became known as the Bash Brothers. Jose possessed a unique blend of speed and power, becoming the first major leaguer to log 40 home runs and 40 stolen bases in a single season.

Unfortunately, he became enamored of the long ball and, in his obsession to reach 500 homers, let the other parts of his game suffer. While with the Red Sox, Canseco took part in a play that has become a mainstay in any baseball blooper collection. Going back on a long fly to right field, he put up his glove, only to have the ball bounce off his head over the fence for a home run. His defensive play became so offensive that Canseco was considered a liability in the field. He played out his last years as a designated hitter for hire, bouncing from team to team. In 2002, no one took him on and he finished 24 long balls short of his 500-homer goal.

Actually, Jose Canseco can be considered a study in misguided faith. His pursuit of 500 home runs at the expense of other parts of his game was akin to worshiping a false god. That he relied on steroids, a banned substance, to bulk up, dishonored the game he played. He stole from himself the wonderful combination of speed and power that was his gift; he buried a talent that was given him.

Canseco could have had a place in the Hall of Fame. Instead the game had no place for him. Though graced with a gift, he fell from baseball's grace.

Even beloved superstars have fallen victim to their own talents. Mickey Mantle played more than 2,400 games, hit 536 home runs, batted .300 or better ten times, appeared in sixteen All-Star games, won the 1956 Triple Crown, and three Most Valuable Player Awards, and helped lead the Yankees to twelve American League pennants and eight World Series titles. Along the way he became an American icon. A switch-hitter with blazing speed and incredible power, Mantle carried the baton, albeit reluctantly, that had been passed from Ruth to Gehrig to DiMaggio to him.

As a young boy from the hard scrabble region of Oklahoma, he suffered from osteomyelitis, a degenerative bone disease. A high school football injury had one doctor ready to amputate Mantle's leg, but the new wonder drug of the day, penicillin, helped clear the infection. In Mantle's first World Series in 1951, he tore cartilage in his knee stopping short so as not to run into Joe DiMaggio as both chased a fly ball in right center field. In Gerald Astor's *The Baseball Hall of Fame 50th Anniversary Book*, Robert Lipsyte wrote that Mantle "rested his bad leg that winter, but never did the prescribed exercises to strengthen it. He would come to regret that later. The muscles deteriorated and his knee was always weak and easily injured."[4]

Between not taking better care of himself and a tendency to drink, Mantle's many talents never fully shined. True, his achievements earned him membership in the Hall of Fame, but he could have done much more. In his own book, *The Mick*, he says,

At the end of the season [1968] my lifetime average had dipped under .300. The most disappointing thing ever. I could hardly stand to think about it. Even after my second year with the Yankees, when I hit .311 and finished third (in batting average) behind Ferris Fain of the A's and Dale Mitchell of Cleveland, even then it was almost impossible to accept. I felt I should've led the league and I only did that once in my major league career. But goddamn, to think you're a .300 hitter and end up at .237 in your last season, then find yourself looking at a lifetime .298 average—it made me want to cry.[5]

Talent, like faith, is about realizing one's potential. Neither comes automatically; yet we have a responsibility to both. For though talent and faith are gifts from God, we must work at reaping their rewards. Each must be an active, living part of our life. By devoting time and study, we hone our talents and increase our faith. Hitters take batting practice, fielders take infield practice. For only by practice can we approach perfection.

In later years, fans of baseball took a new look at Mantle and his accomplishments. His diseased liver, attributed in part to years of alcohol abuse, caused Mantle to admit to his failings and encourage others not to make the same mistakes. His repentance earned him forgiveness and reappreciation from those who followed his career, and recognition and affection from those too young to remember. In a way, Mickey Mantle's talent taught him humility.

It seems there are many things we can learn from the Bible and baseball, not the least of which is the story of the talents. God has granted us our own unique gifts. We may not be able to throw a baseball 98 miles an hour nor hit one 450 feet. But some of us are able to teach, others to heal. There are those of us with abilities to make people laugh or to lend a helping hand. Still others have the faculties to invent, to create, to serve. Above all, we all have the capacity to love—the game of baseball and one another.

"THERE GOES THE GREATEST HITTER WHO EVER LIVED."

What Ted Williams hoped people would say of him[1]

A dispute also arose among them as to which one
of them was to be regarded as the greatest.

LUKE 22:24

BASEBALL IS A GAME OF DIMENSIONS: 60 feet 6 inches from pitching rubber to plate; 90 feet between the bases; 315 feet down the left field line to Fenway Park's Green Monster, which stands 37 feet tall. Our national pastime is also a game of accomplishment: 363 wins by Warren Spahn, the most by a left-handed pitcher in history; Pete Rose's 4,256 hits, the most ever; Cal Ripken, Jr.'s, iron man streak of 2,632 consecutive games played. So it only stands to reason that through computation and comparison, experience and evaluation, that one player would rise among the rest to be proclaimed the greatest, the best there ever was.

Part of what makes baseball great, apart from the game itself, is comparing great players from different eras to arrive at just such a proclamation of who is the best of the best. Babe Ruth never had to play under the lights, hit a slider, or face the specialists of today's bullpens. Hank Aaron had the benefit of hitting in Atlanta's Fulton County Stadium, nicknamed "the launching pad" for its home run friendly atmosphere, whereas Willie Mays played in that cyclone-in-an-ice-box known as Candlestick Park. Ted Williams lost precious years to military service, while Barry Bonds enjoys hitting against expansion team pitching (that is when pitchers actually pitch to him). Cy Young hurled in the dead ball era, and Bob Gibson when the mound was higher than it is today.

Fans being fans, it's only natural to want to see who is the best at what they do. Like it or not, that's why we keep score, tally home runs, figure out batting averages. Even in Jesus' time, the apostles jockeyed for top billing.

James and John, the sons of Zebedee, came forward to him and said to him, "Teacher, we want you to do for us whatever we ask of you." And he said to them, "What is it you want me to do for you?" And they said to him, "Grant us to sit, one at your right hand and one at your left, in your glory" (Mark 10:35–37).

When the ten heard it, they were angry with the two brothers (Matthew 20:24).

Perhaps the other apostles were embarrassed at the brothers' effrontery. (In his gospel, John referred to himself as "the disciple whom Jesus loved.") But it's more likely that they themselves wanted the exalted positions next to Jesus. After all, Luke did report that a *"dispute... arose among them as to which one of them was to be regarded as the greatest"* (22:24).

All of which just goes to show that whether twelve apostles gather, or a dozen Hall of Famers, eventually talk is going to come around to who's number one. In the baseball world at least, a case can be made for several of the game's Giants...and Yankees, Red Sox, and Cardinals.

Ty Cobb, for instance, was considered by many to be the greatest hitter to have ever played. Said Hall of Famer George Sisler,

The greatness of Ty Cobb was something that had to be seen, and to see him was to remember him forever.[2]

To show how impressive Cobb's credentials are, consider this. He was among the first five players ever inducted into the baseball Hall of Fame. In fact, he received the most votes of anyone in that inaugural class, seven more than the Sultan of Swat, Babe Ruth. Cobb hit .300 or better for twenty-three straight seasons, including three in which he topped .400. He led the Tigers to three straight World Series though they never brought home a championship. Most remarkably, his lifetime average (that's lifetime average, mind you) was an incredible .366. Only Cobb's penchant for overaggressive play, his nasty disposition and, to some, a deep prejudice have kept him from being proclaimed as the greatest player ever.

What Ty Cobb was to the American League, second baseman Rogers Hornsby was to the National, both in temperament (ornery) and performance (peerless). The Rajah is the only right-handed hitter to hit over .400 three times, with a twentieth-century record of .424 in 1924. In fact, during the five-year period of 1921–1925, Hornsby hit .402. He won the Triple Crown in 1922 and 1925, and the MVP in 1925 and 1929. He took his St. Louis Cardinals to the World Series in 1926, and repeated the feat with the Chicago Cubs in 1929. For the Cardinals, it was their first world title. His lifetime batting average of .358 is tops in the National League, second only to Cobb's .366 in all of baseball.

Throughout their careers, Joe DiMaggio of the Yankees and Boston's Ted Williams vied for the unofficial title of greatest player in the game. As mentioned, Joltin' Joe compiled a lifetime batting average of .325, won two batting titles, two RBI titles, two home run titles, three MVP awards, and helped the Yankees win nine world championships. Despite missing five seasons due to military service in two wars, Teddy Ballgame (Williams) captured six batting titles, four home run crowns, two Triple Crowns, two MVP awards, and posted a lifetime mark of .344 with 521 home runs. Along the way he helped the Red Sox reach the World Series in 1946. Perennial all-stars, both DiMaggio and Williams are members of the Hall of Fame.

Each had their unique approach to the game that drove them to such lofty heights. For DiMaggio it was perfection: "There is always some kid who may be seeing me for the first or last time. I owe him my best."[3] For Williams, it was greatness: "I wanted to be the greatest hitter who ever lived. A man has to have goals and that was mine, to have people say, 'There goes Ted Williams, the greatest hitter who ever lived.'"[4]

If one season could encapsulate their rivalry it was 1941. That was the year of "The Streak," DiMaggio's 56-game wonder. The Yankee Clipper led the league in RBIs with 125 and hit .357 in leading his team to yet another World Championship. Not to be outdone, the Splendid Splinter led the league in runs, home runs, and batting average. Not just any batting average, mind you, but .406. He was the first person since 1930 to better .400. He was also the last hitter to do so. As remarkable as his season was, Williams lost in the Most Valuable Player voting to DiMaggio, the Streak and another Yankee pennant.

What DiMaggio and Williams were to the 1930s and 1940s, Willie Mays and Hank Aaron were to the 1950s and 1960s. In fact, Mickey Mantle said, "Aaron was to my time what Joe DiMaggio was to the era when he played."[5] Aaron was a lifetime .305 hitter, Mays .302. The Hammer holds the major league record of 755 home runs and 2,297 RBIs to the Say Hey Kid's 660 and 1,903. Both are members of the 3,000 hit club with Aaron surpassing that mark by 771 and Mays by 283.

Aaron won two batting titles to Mays' one; each either tied or led the league in home runs four times. Aaron also has four RBI titles on his side of the ledger. Between them, they played in 41 All-Star games, with the Brave besting the Giant by one appearance.

While Aaron posted better power numbers, Mays had the better all-around game. Mays became the first player in baseball history to steal 300 bases and hit 300 home runs. Willie finished with 338 thefts to Aaron's 240. Mays also holds the major league record for career outfield putouts with 7,095. With all those basket catches, it's no wonder he won twelve Gold Gloves as a center fielder for the New York and then San Francisco Giants. As a member of the Milwaukee and Atlanta Braves, Aaron earned three of the golden mitts.

Where Mays edges Aaron is in the World Series. In 1957, Aaron was part of the World Champion Braves team that defeated the Yankees. That was the same year that he won his only National League Most Valuable Player Award. A year later, both the Braves and the Bronx Bombers were at it again with the Yanks winning the rematch. Mays pulled his MVP/world title combo in 1954 when his Giants swept the Cleveland Indians in the Series defined by "The Catch." He was also a part of the fabled 1951 team that overcame the Dodgers with Bobby Thomson's "shot heard 'round the world," as well as the 1962 San Francisco version, which again prevailed over the Dodgers in a three-game playoff to reach the Series. In each case, the Giants fell in the fall classic to the Yanks. At the end of his career, Mays went to another World Series, this time as a member of the National League champion New York Mets.

One could certainly make the case for Willie Mays' godson being the best to ever play the game. Barry Bonds is the only player to have ever won seven (not five, not six, but seven) Most Valuable Player Awards, two with the Pirates and five with the Giants. No one else has ever won more than three. A Gold Glove left fielder, Bonds was always a respected hitter. But in 2001, he entered into a league of his own, becoming downright feared as he shattered Mark McGwire's single season home run mark with 73. A year later, he became, at thirty-eight, the oldest player in major league history to win a batting title for the first time with a .370 average. He has also joined Aaron and Ruth as the only players to hit 700 or more home runs. In 2002, he finally took a team to the World Series with his Giants losing in seven exciting games to the California Angels. During that same season, he set major league records for intentional passes and walks with 68 and 198, respectively, a measure of how much teams were afraid to pitch to him. When all is said and done, it seems about the only thing Barry Bonds has not done is pitch. (Of course, many of these achievements would come into question should Bonds be convicted of steroid use.)

Which leads us to a member of the first Hall of Fame class, one of the select group called the Five Immortals.

Any conversation (or heated discussion as the case may be) of the greatest player of all time would be incomplete without the inclusion of George Herman Ruth. Number three for the New York Yankees; number one in many fans' hearts. Over twenty-two years, the Babe logged 2,873 hits, 714 home runs and 2,213 RBIs. Now thought of primarily as a power hitter, Ruth's lifetime average was a rather robust .342. Not only that, but he was six times a world champion.

However, what separates the Bambino from every other player is that not only was he an incomparable slugger, he was also an extremely successful pitcher. In his early career he was 94–46 for the Red Sox. Most people don't realize that his winning percentage of .671 is better than Hall of Famers Grover Cleveland Alexander, Christy Matthewson, and Walter Johnson.

In *The Baseball Hall of Fame 50th Anniversary Book*, sportswriter George Vescey wrote:

I think of all the great players of my four decades as a fan and journalist—the smooth DiMaggio, the fluid Mays, the complete Aaron, the forceful Frank Robinson, the gallant Clemente, the graceful Koufax, the turbulent Mantle, the natural Valenzuela, the disciplined Seaver.

Having seen all the great players of the past four decades, I will take the word of my elders that Babe Ruth could pitch and field and throw and run—yes, even run—with the best of them. And I fully accept that the sum of his ability made him the most exciting, the most dominant player the game has ever known.[6]

However, in defining greatness playing baseball is one thing. Living life is another. People appreciated Willie Mays for the boyish enthusiasm he brought to the game, both in a Giants uniform or playing stick ball in the streets of Harlem. A perfectionist in pinstripes, Joe DiMaggio held the world at a distance and died without many close friends. Babe Ruth lived life large on the field and off, often stretching the limits of propriety. Lou Gehrig earned the loved and respect of fans and players alike for the quiet dignity in which he bore the disease that claimed his life. Grover Cleveland Alexander had bouts with alcohol and died in a rented room, alone. For as great as many considered Ty Cobb, just as many thought him to be a mean old man. The anger that fueled his intensity alienated opponents and teammates alike. When he died, only three men of all those who had played beside him attended the funeral.[7]

To live a good life, it's not enough to excel in one's profession. We must also strive to excel as people. To hold others with respect, care, service and love. As Jesus said, *"For what will it profit them if they gain the whole world but forfeit their life?"* (Matthew 16:26).

With this in mind, a case may be made for yet another player on whom we might bestow the title The Greatest, especially with a biblical overlay. The player? Roberto Clemente.

From 1955–1972, Clemente was a proud and graceful fixture at Forbes Field and later Three Rivers Stadium, playing right field for the Pittsburgh Pirates. He was the consummate ballplayer, equally skilled in all phases in the game. He could hit—he batted .300 or higher 13 times, winning four National League batting titles. He could throw—with a rifle for an arm he led the league in outfield assists five times. He could catch—he won twelve Gold Gloves in a row. A twelve-time All-Star, he won the National League MVP in 1966. A true champion, Clemente helped the Pirates to World Series titles in 1960 and 1971, hitting safely in all fourteen Series games in which he played. His effort on the national stage of the 1971 Series was so spectacular he was named MVP, at long last being appreciated by the entire country for his many talents.

Roger Angell wrote of that remarkable performance saying, Clemente played "a kind of baseball that none of us had ever seen before—throwing and running and hitting at something close to the level of perfection."[8]

On the last day of the 1972 season, Clemente collected his 3,000th hit, joining a select fraternity of baseball's best. It was the last hit he would ever get. He died that New Year's Eve in a plane crash en route to deliver food and medical supplies to earthquake--ravaged Nicaragua.

In responding to the request that opened this inning, Jesus spoke to the qualities of greatness, saying, "...whoever wishes to be great among you must be your servant" (Matthew 20:26). In John's Gospel, Christ taught his apostles that, "no one has greater love than this, to lay down one's life for one's friends" (John 15:13).

It was in the service of others that Roberto Clemente died. That the Hall of Fame Pirate was a great ballplayer was secondary to his being a great human being. Of his play he said, "I want to be remembered as a ballplayer who gave all he had to give."[9]

Clemente gave all he had to give...in baseball and in life.

"WORST TO FIRST"

Minnesota Twins of 1990–1991

"The last will be first."

MATTHEW 20:16

AMONG JESUS' MANY PARABLES is the tale of the workers in the vineyard. Some people might see it as a commentary on contract law, a call for unionization, an invitation to the kingdom of heaven, and a treatise on management's prerogative. It's also a preview of baseball's contract squabbles and the 1991 World Series.

Not bad for three paragraphs.

"For the kingdom of heaven is like a landowner who went out early in the morning to hire laborers for his vineyard. After agreeing with the laborers for the usual daily wage, he sent them into his vineyard.

When he went out about nine o'clock, he saw others standing idle in the marketplace; and he said to them, 'You also go into the vineyard, and I will pay you whatever is right.' So they went. When he went out again about noon and about three o'clock, he did the same. And about five o'clock he went out and found others standing around; and he said to them, 'Why are you standing here idle all day?' They said to him, 'Because no one has hired us.' He said to them, 'You also go into the vineyard.'

When evening came, the owner of the vineyard said to his manager, 'Call the laborers and give them their pay, beginning with the last and then going to the first.' When those hired about five o'clock came, each of them received the usual daily wage. Now when the first came, they thought they would receive more; but each of them also received the usual daily wage. And when they received it, they grumbled against the landowner, saying, 'These last worked only one hour, and you have made them equal to us who have borne the burden of the day and the scorching heat.' But he replied to one of them, 'Friend, I am doing you no wrong; did you not agree with me for the usual daily wage? Take what belongs to you and go; I choose to give to this last the same as I give to you. Am I not allowed to do what I choose with what belongs to me? Or are you envious because I am generous?' So the last will be first, and the first will be last.... For many are called, but few are chosen" (Matthew 20:1–16; 22:14).

Many people, especially in our society, find this parable troubling. Taught that an honest day's work earns an honest day's pay, never mind how a union contract might interpret it, we find it difficult to accept the landowner's approach to work and wages. By our thinking, those who work the longest should earn the most.

Ah, this is where the notion of contract law comes into play. Those hired in the morning agreed to work the day for a fixed wage. The workers put in the time, even during the heat of the day, to fulfill their part of the deal; the landowner paid them as promised. It just so happened that the landowner provided the same compensation for all his workers, no matter how many or few hours they worked. If those who worked fewer hours received a denarius, then the first workers reasoned they would be paid in proportion to the hours they toiled. Much to their dismay, this was not the case.

Baseball presents a similar dilemma regarding salaries. Say a player of certain ability, we'll call him Slammer, signs a long-term contract for $5 million a season; he's analogous to the workers hired by the landowner early in the day. Halfway through Slammer's contract, a second player of comparable ability, Bopper, inks a deal for $8 million a year, receiving more due to the inevitable salary escalation. He represents the workers who are hired later in the day. Each player is paid what his contract dictates, but Slammer may be upset at the perceived salary slight. Just as the first workers were upset, Slam might demand a new contract, an extension, a trade, or lose focus on the field because he feels he's being disrespected.

It's a very natural reaction for the early laborers to be angry at their perceived slight. The discrepancy in hours must have seemed unfair. But maybe Jesus is teaching us that life is not fair. People of questionable character reap monetary gain while innocent children die of cancer. A tornado rips one home apart while the house next door remains unscathed. A drunk driver kills a family of four while he himself suffers not a scratch. Though life may not be fair, Jesus assures us that we all have a chance at the same reward: heaven.

Baseball, too, offers examples of the unfairness of life. Promising careers are cut short due to injury. Not every minor league player makes it to "The Show." Not every major league player competes in the playoffs. Journeymen wear World Series rings while established stars do not. To this last point, examine the careers of Hall of Famer Ernie Banks and Don LeJohn.

As we read earlier, Banks played his entire nineteen-year career in the friendly confines of Wrigley Field. Mr. Cub was two-time National League MVP, hit 512 home runs, and was named to the All-Star team 11 times. Yet he never once made it to postseason play. Don LeJohn played just one season of major league ball. He appeared in all of 34 games, never hit a triple or home run, nor stole a base. He scored a grand total of two runs. But he was fortunate enough to appear in a World Series. He is and always will be a world champion, having been a member of the 1965 Dodgers.

If ever there were an early laborer and a worker-come-lately they would be Banks and LeJohn. However, while disappointed at never playing in the fall classic, Ernie Banks rejoiced at the opportunity he was given to play baseball in the first place. Our lives become very unsatisfactory when we start comparing them with those of others. Inevitably, there will be someone who has a better home or car than we do just as we are able to take a nicer vacation than someone else. Life becomes much more enjoyable when we are thankful for the gifts we do have and enjoy them to the fullest.

Jesus' lesson worked, and still works, on a number of levels. For his immediate audience, the original workers represented the Israelites; those hired later, the Gentiles. The landowner was symbolic of the heavenly Father, the denarius (money) the kingdom of heaven. God had made a covenant, a contract, with the people of Israel that they would be his people, and he would be their God. Jesus introduced a new covenant—his death and resurrection would free the world from sin and open the kingdom for all who believed in him. The Jews had "toiled" for hundreds of years in the vineyard while the Gentiles were new to the fold. Yet, God's love is the same for all.

A more modern interpretation is that the vineyard is the world. And the early laborers are those who have come before us. Our parents and grandparents toiled so that we might have a richer life. We in turn work to the best of our ability to make the world a better place for our children and grandchildren. While our work may be hard, it takes on new meaning when done for the love of others. What's more, each of us has a unique contribution to make, and whether we are able to give a little or a lot, all of our efforts are needed for the vineyard to thrive and for our world to grow.

Christ's explanation that the last shall be first, and the first last was not intended to be a reversal of the Jews' favored status, but rather the introduction of our equality in God's eyes, a leveling of the playing field if you will. If first equals last and last equals first, then there is no first or last, only equals.

Likewise, the phrase *"many are called, but few are chosen"* might be considered exclusionary, that the call to join Jesus is made to many, yet few are actually accepted into his Father's house. Reversing the emphasis, though, reveals just the opposite. The Jews, as the Chosen People, are few. Yet the rest of the world is also invited to Christ's banquet. So many are called (the rest of us) and few are chosen (the Jews). Far from being contradictory, the statements are complementary. Instead of feeling like there's no way we will ever attain union with Christ in heaven we are being told that the reward is there for early and late laborers alike.

Now what does baseball teach us about this parable?

In 1990, both the Minnesota Twins and the Atlanta Braves had disappointing seasons, so much so that they each finished last in their respective divisions. The Twins, with only 74 wins, finished 23 games behind the American League pennant-winning A's; the Braves fared even worse, losing 9 more games and finishing 26 games back of eventual World Series champion Cincinnati.

Remarkably, next season both teams completed historic turn-arounds. Each won their division, Atlanta in the National League West by one game over the Dodgers, Minnesota in the American League West by a healthy eight games over the White Sox. This marked the first time in major league history that a team captured the flag a year after finishing in the cellar. Even more unusual was the fact that two teams accomplished the feat in the same year.

Continuing their Cinderella stories, both Minnesota and Atlanta advanced through the playoffs. The Twins took the Toronto Blue Jays four games to one to reach the World Series, while the Braves came back to overtake the Pittsburgh Pirates four games to three, with three of those games being decided by 1–0 scores, and a fourth by the score of 3–2.

Most thought that the Series contestants would be hard pressed to top the excitement generated by the Braves and Pirates in the National League championship round. Yet that's exactly what happened. Atlanta was led by Tom Glavine, John Smoltz, David Justice, and Terry Pendleton; the Twins by Jack Morris, Kirby Puckett, Chili Davis, and Chuck Knoblauch. The Series went seven games, five of which were decided by a single run, three went into extra innings, including games six and seven.

Knotted at three wins apiece, the two teams battled for nine innings in game seven with nothing to show on the scoreboard but eighteen goose eggs. In the bottom of tenth, after ten shutout innings by Twins pitcher Morris, a broken bat double, sacrifice bunt, and bloop hit produced the game's only run, which led to a world championship for the worst-to-first Minnesota Twins.

The last had become first.

Not only that, just four years earlier, the Twins as a franchise had won their first World Series in sixty-three years. In other words, the team went from first in 1987 to worst in 1990 to first a year later.

The first shall be last and the last shall be first.

In the case of the Twins and every World Series winner, there is a little of the parable of the laborers. The amount of work each player performs may differ. A starting second baseman may be expected to play more than a thousand innings, a left-handed relief specialist may log just a fraction of that. Yet their salaries may be comparable. The regular nine and the starting rotation may share the burden of the season, while the pinch hitters and late season call-ups see only spot duty. However, when each member makes key contributions, large and small, all share in the World Series rewards.

What do we learn from baseball about the discrepancy between the many and the few? With the expansion undertaken by baseball over the years, the number of teams in each league increased, thereby decreasing the odds that any one team would win a pennant. To give more teams a chance at glory, and to keep fan interest alive during the latter part of the season, divisional play and subsequent playoffs were introduced. In 1969 each league split into a West and East division; in 1994 each league added a Central. The first realignment generated a championship series for each league, pitting the best of the West against the "beast" from the East. With the addition of a Central division came the introduction of the wild card team. In each league the winners of the three divisions plus the team with the next best record (the wild card) would enter the playoffs. Prior to 1969, only two teams were called to postseason play. From 1969 through 1993, four clubs were called. Since 1994 the number has jumped to eight.

While many are called to compete, few are chosen for the post-season. And only one is crowned champion. But that's per season. Over the long storied and gloried history of the game, many are called to play *and* many are crowned. There's an equality of sorts in that everyone has a chance to be a champion, and most of the major league franchises, at one time or another, have been. (More on this in a later inning/chapter.)

Whether a team is worst or first, first or last, there is a lesson to be learned about faith. True fans will not lose faith in their team; they will not love their team any less for their performance, just as a parent would not love a child any less for a poor report card. That's not to say that fans or parents aren't disappointed, only that the bonds of the relationship, while tested, are not broken. So, too, is our landowner loyal to all of his workers, even those who object to his compensation practices. He abides by his agreement with each of them.

Ours is a contract with God. His covenant with us promises us everlasting life. All we are asked to do is love and serve God and one another. He may expect more from us than he does from others. He may even ask more of us at times than we feel we can give. He may expect more from those he has given much. But he is steadfast in the fact that his reward is available to us all if we hold up our end of the deal.

"I Really Didn't Say Everything I Said."[1]

Yogi Berra

"...for I will give you words and a wisdom that none of your opponents will be able to withstand or contradict."

LUKE 21:15

AS JESUS WAS NEARING THE LAST DAYS of his ministry on earth, he wanted to impress upon his apostles that they would not be left alone, that the Spirit would be guiding them. On several occasions Jesus foretold of the Spirit's presence to come, including the verse above from Luke. In fact, the Apostles were filled with the Holy Spirit on Pentecost as we noted in the Top of the 4th Inning. From Jesus' explanations to them following his resurrection, plus the gifts of understanding and wisdom, clarity and speech, from the Spirit, the Apostles were equipped to spread the Good News of the Lord Jesus Christ.

Then Peter, filled with the Holy Spirit, said to them, "Rulers of the people and elders, if we are questioned today because of a good deed done to someone who was sick and are asked how this man has been healed, let it be known to all of you, and to all the people of Israel, that this man is standing before you in good health by the name of Jesus Christ of Nazareth, whom you crucified, whom God raised from the dead (Acts 4:8–10).

Inspired by the Spirit, Peter described how we are all made well. By his death and resurrection, Christ conquered sin and death; by God's love and mercy we "helpless" men and women are forgiven our sins, and are given the strength to live up to our birthright, that is, being made in the image and likeness of God.

Mark also wrote of Jesus proclaiming the coming of the Spirit, a passage which is called to mind when Paul went before the authorities during his early ministry.

"When they bring you to trial and hand you over, do not worry beforehand about what you are to say; but say whatever is given you at that time, for it is not you who speak, but the Holy Spirit" (Mark 13:11).

To this day, the Spirit is still at work within us, gently guiding us to do God's will if we would only listen. Elijah the prophet stood on the mountain to hear God. He did not hear the Lord in a great and strong wind, nor an earthquake, nor a fire. Only when Elijah was quiet did he hear the Lord in a still, small voice. We, too, must be alert enough to feel the presence of the Spirit from any number of sources—a book, a song, a parent, a friend, listening to our own thoughts, listening to God speaking to us in a still, small voice, even listening for wisdom in baseball.

Just as Scripture dispenses wisdom through prophets, such as Moses, Isaiah, and Elijah, so too does baseball have its sages. Three of the most notable are Casey, Satchel, and Yogi. Though they are not playing the game today, they have left their marks in the record books and, perhaps even more indelibly, in our hearts. From them we learn of the joy, frustration, craziness, and, ultimately, a love of the game.

Casey Stengel played fourteen years in the major leagues, compiled a .284 career average, and played in three World Series (one winner) where he never hit lower than .364. But it was his tenure as manager of the New York Yankees (where he showed the wisdom of Solomon) and New York Mets (where he showed the patience of Job) that brought the "Ol' Perfessor" his greatest accomplishments. From 1949 through 1960, the Yankees, under Casey's direction, won ten American League pennants and seven World Series titles, including an unprecedented five in a row.

Though out of chronological sequence, the following remarks by Casey paint a vivid picture of his playing days:

"My name is Stengel. Take a good look at me because I'm going to be around a long time.[2]...They brought me up to the Brooklyn Dodgers, which at that time was in Brooklyn.[3]...I was such a dangerous hitter, I even got intentional walks in batting practice.[4]...I broke in with four hits and the writers promptly declared they had seen the new Ty Cobb. It took me only a few days to correct that impression."[5]

But Stengel is most remembered for his leadership of the sublime Yankees and the ridiculous Mets. Again, his own words, even out of context, tell the story as only Stengelese can:

"I can make a living telling the truth.[6]...A shave, please, but don't cut my throat. I may want to do it later myself.[7]...The secret to managing a club is to keep the five guys who hate you from the five who are undecided.[8]...Son, we'd like to keep you around this season, but we're trying to win a pennant.[9]...Sometimes, I get a little hard-of-speaking.[10]...I'd love to leave you in, but I got too many married men in the infield.[11]...No one knows this yet, but one of us has just been traded to Kansas City.[12]...Well, I made up my mind, but I made it up both ways.[13]...I'll never make the mistake of being seventy again.[14]

"The only thing worse than a Mets game is a Mets doubleheader.[15]...Look at that guy. He can't hit, he can't run, and he can't throw. Of course, that's why they gave him to us.[16]...If anybody wants me, tell them I'm being embalmed.[17]...It couldn't have been a perfect pitch. Perfect pitches don't travel that far.[18]...I've been in this game a hundred years, but I see new ways to lose I never knew existed before.[19]…We are a much improved ball club; now we lose in extra innings![20]…The trick is growing up without growing old.[21]…Most people my age are dead at the present time.[22]…You could look it up."[23]

Casey even had a thing or two to say about faith and baseball. He once explained his job to a nun with the following: "I'm the fella in charge. It's kinda like being the mother superior."[24] And recalling that John the Baptist's head was presented to King Herod on a silver platter, he described a player's batting stance this way: "He's an unusual hitter. Sometimes he stands up, and sometimes his head is so close to the plate he looks like John the Baptist."[25]

One of the most proficient pitchers to ever play the game was also one of it's most colorful characters. Unfortunately, it was a color of a different kind that caused his debut in the majors to be long overdue. Despite being shunned by major league owners because of the color of his skin, Satchel Paige may have been the best pitcher to ever have played the game. No less a pitching authority than the Cleveland Indians great Bob Feller said, "Paige was the best pitcher I ever saw."[26] Dizzy Dean agreed that Paige was the greatest he ever witnessed, adding that "and I've been looking in the mirror a long time."[27] No less a hitting authority than Joe DiMaggio proclaimed, "After I got that hit off Satchel, I knew I was ready for the big leagues."[28] And Ted Williams flat out stated, "Satch was the best pitcher in baseball."[29]

It's estimated that he pitched in 2,600 games and won more than 2,000 of them. Unlike hurlers in the majors who pitch every fourth day of the season, Paige took the mound three times a week, year round. As a barnstormer, hero of the Negro Leagues, and eventual major leaguer, Satchel's resumé could serve as a model for a Rand McNally atlas: Mobile, Chattanooga, Chicago, Birmingham, Baltimore, Cleveland, Pittsburgh, Bismarck, Kansas City, Trujillo, Guayama, Santo Domingo, New York, Memphis, St. Louis, Greensborough,

Miami, Portland, Harlem, Anchorage, Atlanta, Indianapolis, and Tulsa.

Along the way, facts were embellished in stories that gave way to legends, until the lines were blurred. Sports commentator Bob Costas put it this way:

> Much of what we know about Satchel Paige comes to us by word of mouth, by tales handed down over the years subject to the perspective and storytelling style of the witness. Much of it is undoubtedly true, some of it is probably apocryphal, all of it contributes to his legend as a ballplayer and one-of-kind personality.[30]

Casey Stengel himself said of Paige, "He threw the ball as far from the bat and as close to the plate as possible."[31]

Or as Satchel put it himself: "My pitching philosophy is simple—keep the ball away from the bat.[32]...Just take the ball and throw it where you want to. Home plate don't move.[33]...I use my single windup, my double windup, my triple windup, my hesitation windup. I use my submariner, my sidearmer, and my bat dodger. Man's got to do what he's got to do.[34]...Baseball has turned me from a second class citizen to a second class immortal.[35]...Methuselah was my first bat boy.[36]...Age is a question of mind over matter. If you don't mind, it don't matter.[37]...Work like you don't need the money. Love like you've never been hurt. Dance like nobody's watching.[38]...We don't stop playing because we get old. We get old because we stop playing."[39]

Perhaps the most quotable of all of baseball's philosophers is Lawrence "Yogi" Berra. These days Yogi is better known for his imaginative use of the English language. But in his day, he was a player. Berra captured the American League Most Valuable Player Award three times, was an All-Star catcher for fifteen consecutive seasons, and played in fourteen World Series. All of which contributed to a

Hall of Fame induction. As a manager, Yogi returned to the Series, taking the Yanks there in 1964 and winning it all with the Mets in 1973. Despite his sterling career, what Yogi may be most famous for is his use or misuse of the English language.

Leave it to Casey to put his favorite catcher in perspective: "He talks okay with a bat in his hands. A college education don't do you no good up there.[40]...They say he's funny. Well, he has a lovely wife, a beautiful home, money in the bank, and he plays golf with millionaires. What's so funny about that?"[41]

And now life according to Yogi: "When you come to a fork in the road, take it.[42]...It was hard to have a conversation with anyone, there were too many people talking.[43]...It's déjà vu all over again.[44]...I really didn't say everything I said."[45]

Casey, Satchel, and Yogi. Three sages of the ages, each with a unique view of baseball and the world. Imagine if you will, it's the seventh game of the World Series. The tying and winning runs are on base. The opposing team's best hitter is about to step into the batter's box. Manager Stengel has just made a call to the bullpen to bring in right-hander Paige. Before Satchel throws his first pitch, there's a conference on the mound among the Ol' Perfessor, his new pitcher and his faithful catcher on how to pitch to this guy.

Casey: All right, everybody line up alphabetically according to your height.[46]

Yogi: Pair up in threes.

Satchel: Keep the juices flowing by jangling around gently as you move.[47]

Casey: There comes a time in every man's life, and I've had plenty of them.[48]

Yogi: When you come to a fork in the road, take it.[49]

Satchel: Don't look back. Something might be gaining on you.[50]

Casey: Good pitching will always stop good hitting, and vice versa.[51]

Yogi: Ninety percent of the game is half mental.[52]

Casey: He's the lower intestine.[53]

Satchel: If your stomach disputes you, lie down and pacify it with cool thoughts.[54]

Yogi: You can't think and hit at the same time.[55]

Casey: He's the perdotious quotient of the qualificatilus.[56]

Yogi: It was hard to have a conversation with anyone, there were too many people talking.

Casey: All right, everybody line up alphabetically according to your height.

Yogi: It's déjà vu all over again.

As for the deeper meaning of it all, keep in mind how the Spirit moves us. For instance, on Pentecost, the Holy Spirit descended upon the Apostles allowing them to speak in tongues and be understood by all. Casey, Satchel, and Yogi often spoke in tongue-twisting, language-bending, grammar-defying ways. Yet we all understand what they meant. Which just goes to show that God works in mysterious ways!

"I Wished Harm to Allie Reynolds."

Childhood confession of Doris Kearns Goodwin[1]

He went out to the mountain to pray.

LUKE 6:12

HERE WE ARE IN THE SEVENTH INNING, the stanza during a major league baseball game when it's customary for fans to rise from their seats, stretch their legs and arms, and reenergize themselves to cheer for their team during the final third of the ball game. Fans for the visiting team stretch at the top of the seventh; hometown faithful before the bottom, when tradition calls for the playing and singing of *Take Me Out to the Ball Game.*

Each stadium has its own custom revolving around baseball's ballad. At Wrigley Field, the late Cubs' announcer Harry Caray used to lean out of the booth, microphone in hand, and lead the fanatics in the song. In Milwaukee, home of beer, brats, and the Brewers, the tune is typically followed by *Roll Out the Barrel.* Those in attendance at Seattle's Safeco Field are treated to an encore of *Louie, Louie,* the song made famous by the Kingsmen.

During the "stretch" portion of the game, fans take the time to compare notes: Will Joe Torre bring in Mariano Rivera in the eighth or ninth, or will Dusty Baker go to his bench with a single digit lead and the pitcher coming up third? Will Randy Johnson get his shutout and break the single game strikeout record?

Those in their seats take a deep breath and brace themselves for the game's final nine outs. Fingers are crossed that the bullpen can come through. Eyes are raised heavenward while lips beseech their team to overcome what seems like an insurmountable lead. Those in need of sustenance for the task at hand fortify themselves with popcorn and peanuts, hot dogs and beer.

This slight respite is a fan's chance to step back from the intensity of the game, to gather their thoughts, replenish themselves, and renew their focus for what lies ahead. Players take their own breaks in the action to calm down, refocus, pause for the cause, and resume the game with renewed intensity and enthusiasm. It may be Carlos Beltran calling time out at the plate after a fast ball has jammed him on the hands. It could be Ichiro asking for a break after a swipe of second base.

All of these moments for fans and players alike are, in their own way, forms of prayer.

Prayer can be described as a quieting of the mind, a refocusing of our hearts on God's purpose for us. Prayer is conversation with God. One way to think of our purpose on earth is to be in right relationship with our Creator. And, as with any relationship, bonds are formed through conversation. Prayers can be offerings of thanks, petitions for solace, praise for life, lamentations of grief, requests for understanding, pleas for guidance, or just a friendly hello. In the Old Testament, one of the traditional forms of prayer was the psalms, poetry that was presented to God in song. *Take Me Out to the Ball Game* is a baseball psalm of sorts, a poem sung in joy for the game.

Of course, the seventh inning may be cause for genuine prayers by faithful fans. Doris Kearns Goodwin, in her memoir *Wait Till Next Year*, tells of her many prayers for the Brooklyn Dodgers, all uttered fervently though not necessarily in the spirit that God intended. We pick her up in mid-confession to her parish priest:

"And to whom did you wish harm?"

My scheme had failed. He [the priest] had picked out the one group of sins that most troubled me. Speaking as softly as I could, I made my admission.

"I wished harm to Allie Reynolds."

"The Yankee pitcher?" he asked, surprise and concern in his voice. "And how did you wish to harm him?"

"I wanted him to break his arm."

"And how often did you make this wish?"

"Every night," I admitted, "before going to bed, in my prayers."

"And there were others?"

"Oh, yes," I admitted. "I wished that Robin Roberts of the Phillies would fall down the steps of his stoop, and that Richie Ashburn would break his hand."

"Is there anything else?"

"Yes, I wished that Enos Slaughter of the Cards would break his ankle, that Phil Rizzuto of the Yanks would fracture a rib, and that Alvin Dark of the Giants would hurt his knee." But, I hastened to add, "I wished that all these injuries would go away once the baseball season ended."[2]

Fortunately, the priest advised the young Miss Kearns that all these injuries would sully whatever benefit her beloved Dodgers might gain from the intercessions on their behalf. That victory would be so much sweeter when earned fair and square. Doris saw the advantages in this approach and, sure enough, when da bums finally triumphed in 1955, it was one of the most joyous moments of her entire childhood.

Jesus often needed a seventh inning stretch in his own life. He used periods of prayer to refocus his energies on his mission, to reconnect with his Father, our God. These times must have been tender moments between Father and Son, just as our prayers with God can be intimate conversations between father and child. If the gospels are any indication, there were instances when the Lord felt abandoned and alone, in need of consolation and fortitude.

And after he had dismissed the crowds, he went up the mountain by himself to pray (Matthew 14:23).

In this case, Jesus had just finished feeding the multitude of five thousand with but five loaves and two fish. There are many reasons Christ might have retired to pray. Perhaps preaching to, and feeding, the crowd was emotionally draining. Or maybe he felt flush from the experience or, more likely, pressed upon by the people to do more than he was willing to do at that time. One very real possibility is that the Lord wanted to offer thanks to God for the wonders he was able to work in his Father's name.

In our day and age, think of how besieged an individual is when he or she wins a multimillion dollar lottery, or how a young man is hounded after signing a lucrative pro basketball contract. Calls come pouring in from long-lost relatives, childhood friends, passing acquaintances, stockbrokers, charities, news organizations, you name it. Now imagine how people might react to a man who could cure illness, disease, make the sick well, heal the mentally disturbed, all with a prayer or the touch of a hand.

But now more than ever the word about Jesus spread abroad; many crowds would gather to hear him and to be cured of their diseases. But he would withdraw to deserted places and pray (Luke 5:15–16).

Though divine, Jesus was also very much human. Plus there are only so many hours in the day. Inevitably, he would have needed to get away if only for a moment's peace of mind, so that he could heal another day. Jesus repaired to the wilderness. How often have we found a walk in the woods, a stroll along an ocean beach, a mountain hike, or fly-fishing along a scenic river to be revitalizing. As we've seen, God created the skies and trees and seeds and beasts of the earth. So it's no wonder that God is found in nature. It's also no surprise that the Lord sought him there.

There may come times when we pray for guidance, whether it be in choosing the right career, deciding about a professional opportunity, or wondering if a certain person is our true soul mate. In the following passage, Luke suggests that Christ, too, prayed for wisdom in the selection of his team, the Twelve Apostles.

Now during those days he went out to the mountain to pray; and he spent the night in prayer to God. And when day came, he called his disciples and chose twelve of them, whom he also named apostles: Simon, whom he named Peter, and his brother Andrew, and James, and John, and Philip, and Bartholomew, and Matthew, and Thomas, and James son of Alphaeus, and Simon, who was called the Zealot, and Judas son of James, and Judas Iscariot, who became a traitor (Luke 6:12–16).

One of Christ's shortest prayers was, for us, his most powerful. *"Father, forgive them; for they do not know what they are doing"* (Luke 23:34). Jesus was on the cross, in the process of being crucified, when he uttered these words to his Father, seeking forgiveness of those thieves who were being crucified with him, forgiveness of the soldiers who divided his garments by casting lots, forgiveness of those who rebuked him, of those who sentenced him and put him to death, and ultimately forgiveness of those of us among his flock, who do not know, who are slow to realize, the errors of our ways.

In a Garden the night before he died, the Lord uttered one of his most well-known prayers:

They went to a place called Gethsemane; and he said to his disciples, "Sit here while I pray." He took with him Peter and James and John, and began to be distressed and agitated. And said to them, "I am

deeply grieved, even to death; remain here, and keep awake."
And going a little farther, he threw himself on the ground and prayed
that, if it were possible, the hour might pass from him. He said,
"Abba, Father, for you all things are possible; remove this cup from
me; yet, not what I want, but what you want" (Mark 14:32–36).

Even Jesus had moments of distress, times of trouble. Was he looking to escape the ordeal and certain death before him? You bet. Did he pray for this petition to be granted? Yes and no. While Christ asked his Father to spare him of what was to come, Jesus knew that we are all here on this earth to do God's will, even if that will may be contrary to ours. So while this prayer was one of petition, it was also one of affirmation of Christ's fidelity to his Father.

As with any form of conversation, prayer is equal parts speaking and listening. For most of us, it's easy to do the talking. We ask God for help, forgiveness, understanding, consolation. We give thanks for our children, a sunset, a recovery, a home team victory.

But should we pray to God for guidance of one sort or another, how would we know which way God would have us turn? This is where quiet meditation and reflective prayer come in to play. It is only when we are silent, when we silence the noise around us, that we can hear God's reply.

When Jesus prayed, he knew how important it was to listen to his Father. This is how he came to know his Father, that in some mysterious way he and the Father were one with the Spirit at the same time as Christ was wholly human.

The words that I say to you I do not speak on my own; but the
Father who dwells in me does his works (John 14:10).

Jesus, the Word made flesh, learned how our relationship with the Father would be forged by prayer.

"Ask, and it will be given you; search, and you will find; knock, and the door will be opened for you. For everyone who asks receives, and everyone who searches finds, and for everyone who knocks, the door will be opened. Is there anyone among you who, if your child asks for bread, will give a stone? Or if the child asks for a fish, will give a snake? If you then, who are evil, know how to give good gifts to your children, how much more will your Father in heaven give good things to those who ask him! (Matthew 7:7–11).

As for how we should lead our lives, Jesus learned of that also.

"Therefore do not worry, saying, 'What will we eat?' or 'What will we drink?' or 'What will we wear?' For it is the Gentiles who strive for all these things; and indeed your heavenly Father knows that you need all these things. But strive first for the kingdom of God and his righteousness, and all these things will be given to you as well.

"So do not worry about tomorrow, for tomorrow will bring worries of its own. Today's trouble is enough for today" (Matthew 6:31–34).

"But I say to you that listen, love your enemies, do good to those who hate you, bless those who curse you....Give to everyone who begs from you....Do to others as you would have them do to you.... Be merciful, just as your Father is merciful" (Luke 6:27, 30–31, 36).

Like Christ, we too can use prayer as a time to tune out the world around us and refocus on our spiritual task at hand. The key though is to treat prayer as a conversation with our God. And like all good conversations, prayer involves the sharing of our most intimate feelings as well as listening. In baseball, we listen to coaches and to broadcasts to learn how the game is played. By "listening" to the word of God in the Bible, we learn how life is to be lived.

"WILLIE, MICKEY, AND THE DUKE"

Lyric from "Talkin' Baseball" by Terry Cashman[1]

The Father, Son, and Holy Spirit.
THE THREE PERSONS OF THE BLESSED TRINITY

ASK ANY GROUP OF FANS WHY THEY LIKE the game of base-ball and chances are you'll receive as many different answers as the number of people you question. There are those who love the long ball and others who appreciate a pitchers' duel. Some will fondly recall how a day at the ball park reminds them of playing catch with their dads summers long ago. Others are enamored of the chesslike moves managers make late in the game. And still others just enjoy the opportunity for a cold beer on a warm night under the lights.

If you were to continue your survey and inquire how people view God, you'd likewise receive a wide range of responses. Some people are in awe of the powerful force that is the source of all creation. Others find great comfort in the merciful God who constantly for-gives us our sins. Still others find it easier to relate to Jesus because he shares our human experience.

There is no right or wrong way to experience baseball or faith. Joy can be found in seeing your first baseball game or your thou-sandth, from watching fireworks after a home run or understanding the infield fly rule. There is wonder to be experienced in seeing God in the delicate nature of a flower or the vastness of the cosmos, the smile from a child's face or the gratitude that comes from serving others.

As our knowledge and appreciation of faith and baseball deepen, we find that we are continually rewarded with blessings from each. Thus our task becomes finding those ways in which we are best able to relate to the game and our God.

Which brings us to the gifted baseball threesome of Willie, Mickey, and the Duke, and the Blessed Trinity of the Catholic faith—Father, Son, and Holy Spirit. Each of these six persons provides a different way to come to know the beauty of a much loftier notion.

Willie, Mickey, and the Duke were three of the most talented center fielders to ever play the game. The mere mention of their names conjures up heroic accomplishments. Mays' dramatic catch of Vic Wertz's line drive in the 1954 World Series, called by many the greatest catch ever made. Mantle's mammoth 565-foot home run against the Washington Senators, the longest recorded home run ever hit. Duke Snider helping lead the Dodgers to the only World Series title Brooklyn was to ever know.

What made their rivalry so exciting was the stage—New York City, home to commerce and culture, skyscrapers and subways and, most importantly, to three major league baseball teams. That there were three teams in New York during the 1950s might be expected, but that each possessed a superbly talented outfielder was beyond even the wildest New Yorker's dreams.

Pulitzer Prize-winning historian Doris Kearns Goodwin recalls what a glorious time it was in her memoir *Wait Till Next Year*, a heartfelt recollection of growing up Catholic and a Dodger fan in Brooklyn in the 1950s:

> For all of us, the love was personal and familiar. We spent hours arguing about whether Duke Snider, Willie Mays, or Mickey Mantle was the best center fielder. The handsome, smooth-fielding Duke Snider was the most consistent home-run hitter of the three, but Mays had a balletic grace and a

joyful fury, while the switch-hitting Mantle had the greatest raw power and speed.[2]

Willie, Mickey, and the Duke. Each not so much played center field as performed there; each provided the power that drove their teams to greatness. Mays' Giants, Mantle's Yankees, and Snider's Dodgers battled one another in New York's private version of King of the Hill, while the rest of baseball and the nation watched in amazement. Whether seeing the outfielders in person or watching them on television, listening to their exploits on the radio, or reading about them three thousand miles away, for a follower of the game it was as close to heaven as an earthbound fan could get.

In the seven years (1951–1957) that the trio patrolled their respective pastures in New York, two of their three teams faced each other in the World Series six times. In that span, the Giants won two National League pennants and one World Series, the Dodgers four National League flags and one Series title, and the Yankees six American League pennants and four championships.

Batting from the right side, Mays averaged .311 in batting, with 31 home runs and 84 RBIs for those seven seasons (even though he lost nearly two years to military service). Hitting from the left side, Snider averaged .305, nearly 37 home runs and 111 runs batted in. While the switch-hitting Mantle compiled an average of .316, 30 homers, and 96 RBIs. Each player was a home run champion. Mays and Mantle topped their leagues in batting; Snider and Mantle in RBIs. Willie and Mickey were Most Valuable Players. Mantle won the Triple Crown.

But the numbers only tell part of the story; their allure was also in the way they played the game. Here's what Hall of Famer Stan Musial, he of the seven National League batting titles, said of Mays:

Willie ranks with DiMaggio as the best I ever saw. He's a perfect ballplayer, too. Mays can beat a ball club with his bat, his glove, his arm, and his legs. He has stolen more bases than any other home-run hitter who ever lived and hit more homers than any base-stealer, past or present. The guy plays with a contagious enthusiasm. Why he can run better and faster looking back over his shoulder to see where the ball is, than most players can digging for the next base with [their] head down.[3]

Robert Lipsyte, on the other hand, sang Mickey Mantle's praises:

He could, with the exquisite delicacy of a surgeon, drag a bunt, then beat it out with sprinter's speed. He could blast a line drive into the outfield, and take an extra base. He could bludgeon the ball—the baseball jumped off his bat, old-timers liked to say—farther than anyone else; the so-called tape-measure home run was a Mantle specialty.[4]

Or as Casey Stengel put it: "He has more speed than any slugger, and more slug than any speedster."[5]

As for the Duke of Flatbush, Roger Kahn rhapsodized about Snider in *The Boys of Summer* and *Memories of Summer*:

Edwin Donald Snider was the full name, but Duke suited. His hair had started graying when he was twenty-five, but his body bespoke supple youth. As Duke moved in his long-striding way, one saw the quarterback, the basketball captain, the Olympian. *Yours is the Earth and everything that's in it.* "If" was a perfect poem for the Duker. He and Kipling would have been to one another's taste.[6]

He had hit 407 home runs, more than any Dodger, more than all but about a dozen men in baseball history.[7]

Center field belonged to Snider, rangy and gifted and supple, Duke could get his glove thirteen feet into the air.

The center field wall was cushioned with foam rubber, and Snider, in pursuit of high drives, ran at the wall, dug a spiked shoe into the rubber and hurled his body upward. Pictures of him in low orbit survive.[8]

Beyond individual statistics and team accomplishments, what each of the center fielders did in unique fashion was expose a city and a country to baseball. By their grace and power, the players offered fans, old and young alike, a gateway into the wonders of the game. Taken individually, Willie, Mickey, and the Duke fostered team loyalty and borough allegiance. But taken collectively, the players inspired an appreciation and love of the game itself. In the larger scheme, it didn't matter which player fans cheered. It only mattered that they cheered.

So it is with God.

One of our primary quests in life is to find ourselves in right relationship with God. However, God is unfathomable; we can never comprehend the entity that the Bible describes as "I AM." So we look for ways that we can relate to the Almighty given our human limitations. We may find God in the beauty of a sunset or the joy of a child's laugh. We may relate to the "Force Be with You" or pray to the three persons of the Blessed Trinity.

The Blessed Trinity is one of the most recognized and least understood concepts within the Catholic faith. Simply put, the Holy, or Blessed Trinity, is three persons—Father, Son, and Holy Spirit—in one God.

Far be it from me to try to explain in a few paragraphs what theologians have devoted the better part of two millennia trying to understand. Three distinct persons in the same one God is a mystery to be sure. But it is also a blessing. For in each of the three persons, we have the opportunity to come to know the one God better. In God the Father, we pray to the Creator of all that is. Through God the Son, we are able to forge a relationship with Jesus who walked the earth and died for our sins. Through the Spirit, comes all our awareness of God and his love for us.

There are a number of references in Scripture that reveal the unique relationship of these persons to one another.

And Jesus came and said to them, "All authority in heaven and on earth has been given to me. Go therefore and make disciples of all nations, baptizing them in the name of the Father and of the Son and of the Holy Spirit... (Matthew 28:18–19).

When Jesus was baptized by John the Baptist in the Jordan River, all three Persons of the Trinity were present.

In those days Jesus came from Nazareth of Galilee and was baptized by John in the Jordan. And just as he was coming up out of the water, he saw the heavens torn apart and the Spirit descending like a dove on him. And a voice came from heaven, "You are my Son, the Beloved; with you I am well pleased" (Mark 1:9–11).

Don't worry if you have trouble grasping the concept of the Blessed Trinity. After all, Jesus' own disciples, men who had been with him day in and day out, did not fully understand.

Philip said to him, "Lord, show us the Father, and we will be satisfied." Jesus said to him, "Have I been with you all this time, Philip, and you still do not know me? Whoever has seen me has seen the Father. How can you say, 'Show us the Father'? Do you not believe that I am in the Father and the Father is in me? The words that I say to you I do not speak on my own; but the Father who dwells in me does his works. Believe me that I am in the Father and the Father is in me; but if you do not, then believe me because of the works themselves (John 14:8–11).

There are times in our lives when we pray to God by way of each person of the Trinity, instances when each person offers a gateway to God. At the birth of a child, ecstatic parents thank creator God profusely for the miracle they hold in their hands. At times of temptation or frustration, we may pray to Jesus for the strength to endure the human journey, knowing that Christ faced most of the same experiences we do. When seeking how to best serve God with the talents he has given us, we seek guidance from the Spirit. In each case we converse with a distinct person of the Trinity at the same time we forge a relationship with God.

To grasp the Trinity, think back to the three outfielders. One position, three players. Each allowed the baseball faithful entrée to the grace of the game. Each possessed unique gifts. Willie, Mickey, and the Duke offered fans everywhere three different ways to embrace the game, just as Father, Son, and Holy Spirit offer the faithful three distinct ways to relate to the one, same God.

After all, whether it's the bottom of the ninth or the end of the world, it's not so much how we have come to believe, it's that we do believe.

"I HAVE LONG AGO FORGIVEN HIM, AND I REALLY HOPE HE HAS FORGIVEN ME."1

Juan Marichal on John Roseboro

"For if you forgive others their trespasses,
your heavenly Father will also forgive you."
MATTHEW 6:14

ONE OF THE MOST IMPORTANT LESSONS Christ gave to his disciples was the concept of forgiveness. Jesus' ultimate reason for coming into the world was to die for our sins, gaining for us the perpetual forgiveness of the Father. In his dying, Christ conquered sin and death; in his living he showed us the way to the kingdom of heaven. To follow Jesus was, simply, to forgive, a notion he learned from the Father.

> *For your Father knows what you need before you ask him.*
> *"Pray then in this way:*
> *Our Father in heaven,*
> *hallowed be your name.*
> *Your kingdom come.*
> *Your will be done,*
> *on earth as it is in heaven.*
> *Give us this day our daily bread.*

And forgive us our debts,
as we also have forgiven our debtors.
And do not bring us to the time of trial,
but rescue us from the evil one.

For if you forgive others their trespasses, your heavenly Father will
also forgive you; but if you do not forgive others, neither will your
Father forgive your trespasses" (Matthew 6:8–15).

Debts. Trespasses. In a word, sins. That comprehensive, some-times nebulous, category of our thoughts and actions that create a distance in our loving relationship with our Father and one another. Fortunately, God loves us so much, he continually forgives us of our wrongdoings. Through that mercy, we come to know his love. In the same way that God forgives us, we too are to pardon others. Christ elaborates in the following from Mark and Luke.

"Whenever you stand praying, forgive, if you have anything against
anyone; so that your Father in heaven may also forgive you your
trespasses" (Mark 11:25–26).

"Do not judge, and you will not be judged; do not condemn,
and you will not be condemned. Forgive, and you will be forgiven"
(Luke 6:37).

That's not to say forgiving is easy. While perhaps grasping the notion of forgiveness, the Apostles failed, if Peter is any indication, to understand the all-encompassing concept of Forgiveness. That is, to forgive time and time again until the end of time.

Then Peter came and said to him, "Lord, if another member of the
church sins against me, how often should I forgive? As many as
seven times?" Jesus said to him, "Not seven times, but, I tell you,
seventy-seven times" (Matthew 18:21–22).

In the Bible, the number seven equals more than a quantity between six and eight; it conveys abundance. So by forgiving someone seven times, Peter felt he was being more than generous. Christ's reply of *"seventy-seven"* is the equivalent to infinity times infinity (to me this emphasizes the incredible number of times we're to forgive).

Why forgiveness?

Forgiveness is the tie that binds. It closes distances and heals wounds. It liberates one from anxiety and sorrow; it frees the other from anger, bitterness, and revenge. Imagine if the Israelis and Palestinians responded to one another with apologies instead of bullets, amends instead of bombs.

Forgiveness also paves the way for our relationship with God. It is the bridge between our inherent failings as humans and the perfection that is the Almighty. Only through God's love and forgiveness can we consider ourselves worthy of being one with the Father in heaven.

Baseball certainly knows of man's propensity to err. Errors are part of the game. Even if fans are slow to forgive a player's miscue, players realize that they are human and are prone to mistakes. It was Jesus who in effect said, *"Let anyone among you who is without sin be the first to throw a stone."* Every ballplayer knows he, too, will make an error sometime. Pittsburgh Pirate first baseman Dick Stuart even made a name for himself for his "mitts-adventures"—Dr. Strangeglove.

Errors don't just happen in the field either. Batters miss signs, runners get picked off base. The great Babe Ruth himself ended the 1926 World Series by being thrown out trying to steal second base in the bottom of the ninth inning of the seventh and deciding game against the Cardinals. It should be noted that he represented the tying run.

Hitters make mistakes, too. Rallies are killed with a weak pop up, a double play ball, a strike out. Heck, Mickey Mantle whiffed 1,710 times, Bobby Bonds 1,757, and Reggie Jackson 2,597. In Jackson's case, that's the equivalent of four full seasons of never hitting the ball.

Baseball also knows of the need for forgiveness. If grudges were carried from game to game, season to season, teams would quickly break into factions, divided against one another, instead of being unified in pursuit of their common goal of winning. How simple it is for the author of an errant throw to say, "My fault." How much of a relief it is to hear in return, "No sweat, you'll get 'em next time." Would that we at home and workplace could be as contrite, that we in schoolyard and political arena could be as forgiving.

How important is forgiveness? During his ministry, Jesus became known as a wonder worker, a miracle man. So much so that people lost sight of the lessons to be learned. To impress upon his followers the magnitude of forgiving, Jesus often placed a greater emphasis on it than the miracles themselves.

Just then some men came, carrying a paralyzed man on a bed. They were trying to bring him in and lay him before Jesus; but finding no way to bring him in because of the crowd, they went up on the roof and let him down with his bed through the tiles into the middle of the crowd in front of Jesus. When he saw their faith, he said, "Friend, your sins are forgiven you." Then the scribes and the Pharisees began to question, "Who is this who is speaking blasphemies? Who can forgive sins but God alone?" When Jesus perceived their questionings, he answered them, "Why do you raise such questions in your hearts? Which is easier, to say, 'Your sins are forgiven you,' or to say, 'Stand up and walk'? But so that you may know that the Son of Man has authority on earth to forgive sins"—he said to the one who was paralyzed—"I say to you, stand up and take your bed and go to your home." Immediately he stood up before them, took what he had been lying on, and went to his home, glorifying God (Luke 5:18–25).

While there are many references in the Bible regarding the importance and power of forgiveness, all one really needs to know is the story of Jesus and Peter. Not to mention the baseball tale of Juan and John.

Recall that, despite Christ's foretelling, Peter denied his Lord three times, an episode that exemplifies our own tendency to fail repeatedly despite our best intentions. Though a low point in Peter's life, the event provided Jesus with an opportunity to demonstrate God's forgiveness of each of our debts, of every trespass, of all of our sins.

When they had finished breakfast, Jesus said to Simon Peter, "Simon son of John, do you love me more than these?" He said to him, "Yes, Lord; you know that I love you." Jesus said to him, "Feed my lambs." A second time he said to him, "Simon son of John, do you love me?" He said to him, "Yes, Lord; you know that I love you." Jesus said to him, "Tend my sheep." He said to him the third time, "Simon son of John, do you love me?" Peter felt hurt because he said to him the third time, "Do you love me?" And he said to him, "Lord, you know everything; you know that I love you." Jesus said to him, "Feed my sheep" (John 21:15–17).

Three times did Peter deny Jesus; three times did Christ welcome him home. So, too, will he welcome us home if only we but knock at his door and say, "My fault."

One might expect forgiveness on the Sea of Galilee. After all, Jesus is divine. He is above pettiness and holding a grudge. His mercy has no end. But what about forgiveness on the fields of play? At the offices of work? In the rooms of home? Many times we are so wounded by another that we are left with physical or emotional scars, anger, or thoughts of vengeance.

As to how to deal with hurts such as these, we can turn once again to baseball.

One of the most heated, some say hated, rivalries in all of sport is between the Giants and Dodgers. Both clubs battled each other while in New York, and then transplanted their bitter relationship when each team moved to the West Coast for the 1958 season. In 1951 and again in 1962, the teams battled in a three-game playoff to determine which club would go to the World Series. In both cases, the Giants won the deciding third game. Each team has taken delight in keeping the other from postseason play on the last game of the season. On the last weekend of the 1982 season, each team knocked the other out of contention on successive days.

However, one event seemed to define the hostility these two teams have had for each other. It was quite possibly the ugliest brawl to ever take place between the lines. During an August game in the summer of 1965, Giant pitcher Juan Marichal had been aggressive in pitching the Dodger batters inside. Dodger catcher John Roseboro took exception to that tactic and, when Marichal himself was batting, threw a ball back to the mound that reportedly nicked the Giant player in the ear. In response, Marichal turned on Roseboro, swinging his bat at the catcher. Before the two were separated, Roseboro's face was bloodstained, the result of a two-inch gash on his forehead.

If ever there was an incident in baseball where forgiveness would be difficult, this was it. Being attacked by a thrown ball, or worse a swung bat, goes beyond competitiveness and becomes a criminal assault. It would have been quite easy for Marichal, whose inclusion into the Hall of Fame was believed to be held up because of this incident, to be bitter. It would have been perfectly understandable for Roseboro to feel aggrieved and hold a grudge.

But baseball, and life, is full of surprises.

By the late 1990s, John Roseboro had been battling the effects of a series of strokes for years, and had sequestered himself away from friends, teammates, the world. It was only when his wife, Barbara, sought the aid of fellow Dodgers did Rosie rebound. In the following, *Los Angeles Times* sportswriter Bill Plaschke captures a side of baseball seldom seen by the everyday fan, a side of friendship, loyalty, support, love and, yes, forgiveness.

"THANK YOU, MASKED MAN..."

What Juan Marichal's bat couldn't do, the fury of two blood clots did.

There lay the toughest Los Angeles Dodger catcher two weeks ago, the sudden victim of two strokes, barely able to speak, still trying to call the game.

"I'm done," John Roseboro mumbled to his wife and daughter. "I'm done."

Three years with a failing heart had sapped his strength. Three years of seclusion in his basement had flat-lined his perspective. This latest squealing ride to Cedars-Sinai had stolen his will.

Once the emotional core of a Dodgers team that was beloved by millions, John Roseboro, sixty-nine, had quit, surrounded by a cheering section that numbered two.

"He wanted to leave us," said his wife Barbara Fouch-Roseboro. "This was the end."

Then it wasn't. Something had blocked the catcher's path.

The doctors say it was science. His family believes it was 1960s Dodgers chemistry.

Those teammates from whom he had hidden in embarrassment over his feebleness were contacted by a stubborn wife who decided her husband needed their love.

And so they emerged from the shadows with a dugout full of it.

"It was everybody he once stood up for, standing up for him," Barbara said.

It was Peter O'Malley sending prayers over a cell phone. It was Tommy Davis sending messages through a nurse's station. It was Maury Wills on one line, Sandy Koufax on another.

It was thoughts and strength from some of this franchise's most glorious moments.

And even one of their darkest.

John Roseboro's cry for help eventually spanned a continent, reaching a phone in the Dominican Republic. "Please tell John to hang on," Juan Marichal said. "Please tell him I'm praying for him."

Today John Roseboro is still hospitalized, still suffering from a failing heart and stroke-impeded speech. But his condition is stable. And after three years of hiding, he is again among friends. "An amazing thing, against the odds, he's still hanging in there," Barbara said between her calls on her cell phone in the hospital cafeteria. "And I think I know why."

Koufax sent a quip:

"Tell John he didn't make much sense even before the stroke."

Marichal sent a bombshell:

"What John did for me, I will never forget."

It was supposed to be the other way around. What Marichal did to Roseboro at Candlestick Park on August 22, 1965, was something that Roseboro was never supposed to forget.

Irritated that Marichal had brushed back two fellow Dodgers hitters that day, Roseboro retaliated while Marichal was batting.

After catching an inside fast ball from Koufax, he directed his return throw near Marichal's face, allegedly nicking his ear.

Marichal spun and began beating Roseboro's head with the bat, raising a giant lump and causing a two-inch gash from which blood poured down his face. It was the most violent incident in Dodger history and the most heated moment of one of baseball's best rivalries.

It was also the defining moment of Roseboro's career. But for reasons you'd never imagine.

Seventeen years later, after failing to be elected to the Hall of Fame in his first two years of eligibility, Marichal was worried that voters were biased against him because of the incident.

So he phoned Roseboro, who had barely spoken to him since that game.

Marichal wanted Roseboro to publicly forgive him, hopefully convincing voters that he should be allowed into the Hall of Fame.

"John couldn't see any reason not to forgive," Barbara said. "He wanted the pain of that day to go away."

Roseboro not only agreed, he flew to the Dominican Republic to play in Marichal's golf tournament and show the baseball world that they were friends.

A couple of months later, in 1983, Marichal phoned again. This time, he was crying.

"He had just been elected to the Hall of Fame, and all he could say was, 'Thank you, thank you, thank you,'" Barbara said.

Reached by phone about Roseboro's illness last week, Marichal's voice broke again.

"A wonderful, wonderful man," he said. "I have long ago forgiven him, and I really hope he has truly forgiven me."[2]

Jesus forgave Peter. John forgave Juan. Peter, for all his stubbornness and foibles, was handpicked to lead Christ's Church. Marichal, despite his attack on Roseboro, was voted into Cooperstown. If not greatness then we may find peace of mind waiting for us if we but seek or grant forgiveness, if we are given a second chance.

In faith as in baseball, forgiveness is an integral part of the healing that needs to occur for all of us to be brought closer together. Perhaps we can all learn from Jesus Christ and John Roseboro. Maybe we can all learn to forgive one another.

After all, as the Boston Red Sox team celebrated their first World Series win in eighty-six years, finally removing the Curse of Babe Ruth, I saw two fans walking around Busch Stadium with a bed-sheet sign. On it were painted words that washed away a certain fielding miscue of the 1986 Series: We forgive Bill Buckner.

Top of the 9th

"ANSWERED PRAYERS! AFTER 42 YEARS, THE ANGELS WIN THE SERIES"

Cover Headline, Sports Illustrated, November 4, 2002[1]

"And your children shall be shepherds in the wilderness for forty years...."

NUMBERS 14:33

GOD IS ETERNAL, ALWAYS WAS, ALWAYS WILL BE. When Moses asked God who he should say is sending him to see Pharaoh, the Almighty one replied, I AM WHO I AM (Exodus 3:14). In other words, I am the one who is and who always has been. Another way to consider this chronological conundrum is that God is the eternal now. Always present. So it should come as no surprise that God is on a different clock than we are. If we equate the lore of Genesis with the discoveries of science, one day of God's time equals billions of years of ours. All this is to say that while forty years may seem like half a lifetime to us, it's just an instant to God, a single foul ball in the history of baseball.

That's not to say that forty years is insignificant to God...or forty days for that matter. Forty is a significant number in the Bible.

And the Spirit immediately drove him out into the wilderness. He was in the wilderness forty days, tempted by Satan... (Mark 1:12–13).

Perhaps it took that long for Jesus to truly discern his ministry, to delve into the depths of his relationship with the Father, to find the inner strength to stand up to Satan, the Pharisees, Pilate, and ultimately the cross.

In the Old Testament, it took forty years for Moses to lead God's Chosen People to the Promised Land. Some biblical authors saw those years as a test.

Remember the long way that the LORD your God has led you these forty years in the wilderness, in order to humble you, testing you to know what was in your heart, whether or not you would keep his commandments (Deuteronomy 8:2).

Though the Jews continued to wander while generations passed away and new ones were born, God did not forsake his people. It is said that God answers our prayers in his own way, in his own time. So it was with Moses and his masses. Before the Jews were allowed possession of a land of their own, they had to wander for forty years. As they searched for their place in the world, God allowed them the time to find him in their hearts. As the Chosen People, the twelve tribes were tested; they had to prove their love and allegiance to God, the Father. Finally, they had to wage battle against the evil Canaanites before they could rightfully inherit, and inhabit, the land of Canaan, their promised land.

All too often time is our best teacher. For one thing, we do not know everything at the outset. We learn from experience. We take time to think things over before making an important decision. For some it may take the modern-day equivalent of forty days to decide to make an investment, buy a home, make up with a spouse or sibling. For others it has taken forty years or longer to find their true passion, whether as a person or in a profession. Far from being a test of our patience, time provides us wisdom that comes from enduring temptation or trial. It grants us the opportunity to grow into the person, community, world, that resides at the other side of our potential.

To help us pass this test of time, we would do well to learn from the game of baseball. Many are the teams that wander the wilderness as seasons pass them by, enduring long hot summers, ill-timed injuries, ill-fated trades, heartbreaking losses. Players and fans wonder when, or if, they will ever see the promised land of a World Series championship.

Forty years may seem like a long time for wandering. In fact, some may scoff at the idea. But if baseball is any kind of reflection of faith, we find that it's not unusual to wait four decades, or longer, for deliverance. The Astros, Brewers, Expos/Nationals, Mariners, Padres, Rangers, Rockies, and Devil Rays have been waiting their entire existences to win a World Series. Four of those teams have never appeared in the fall classic. Texas has been wandering for forty-plus years, which gives new meaning to the term "Lone Star State."

California's Angels claimed their first world title in 2002, after forty-two years as spectators. Just as Moses did not live to see the Promised Land, so too did owner Gene Autry pass on before the pennant was won. Paradoxically, Autry's missing out on the celebration made those present cherish the team's accomplishment all the more.

However, Baltimore's Orioles saw sixty-six years pass by before the Robinson boys, Frank and Brooks, led them to their world title in 1966. Cleveland was last called champion in 1948 thanks to the efforts of Lou Boudreau, Larry Doby, Bob Lemon, and an older fellow by the name of Satchel Paige. For their part, it took the A's forty-two years and playing in three different cities from their 1930 championship in Philadelphia with Al Simmons and pitchers Lefty Grove and George Earnshaw to their three world champion Oakland teams in 1972–1974, featuring Catfish Hunter, Rollie Fingers, and surprise Series star, Gene Tenace. And lest we forget, after the Washington Senators of Walter Johnson, Bucky Harris, and Goose Goslin captured the classic in 1924, it took that franchise sixty-three years, and a different town, to win another Series, this time featuring Frank Viola and Kirby Puckett as the 1987 Twins of Minnesota.

Not to be outdone, the National League boasts its own wandering tribes. Though the Braves have moved three times, they have at least rewarded their fans in each city with a world championship. It's just that it took forty-three years from winning in Boston in 1914 with Johnny Evers, Hank Gowdy, and Rabbit Maranville, to doing the same in Milwaukee in 1957, compliments of Lew Burdette, Warren Spahn, Hank Aaron, and Eddie Mathews. Another thirty-eight years passed until a Brave new World Series dawned in Atlanta behind the pitching of Tom Glavine, Steve Avery, and Greg Maddux.

In a tale of two cities, the Giants kept their New York fans in suspense from 1922, when they won their second consecutive World Series behind the hitting of Frankie Frisch and Irish Meusel, until 1954, when Willie Mays' incredible catch spurred the club to capture the Series flag. Despite three subsequent visits to the classic, the team and its fans have arrived at a fifty-one-year hiatus for a World Series pennant to fly over the city by the Bay. Speaking of New York, across the borough bridge, Brooklyn waited fifty-five years between world titles, winning in 1900 as the Superbas, and then in 1955 as the Dodgers, with the boys of summer, Campanella, Snider, Reese, Robinson, Hodges, Labine, and Podres at long last shining bright. Even one of baseball's most storied franchises has had a significant interval between titles. With their 2006 World Series win, the St. Louis Cardinals now have flown high ten times, yet it took the Redbirds forty-six years before they first took off.

Still, all of the above wandering in the World Series wilderness can't match the hapless drifting of four teams: the Phillies, White Sox, Red Sox, and Cubs. These teams truly realize what it is like to be lost in the desert. Their fans know what it is to have their faith tested season after season.

First, the Phils. It might seem odd that the Phillies are included in this forlorn group. After all, many fans remember their World Series triumph in 1980, when lefty Steve Carlton, catcher Bob Boone and infielders Pete Rose, Larry Bowa, and Mike Schmidt put the love in the brotherly city.

It's the prequel to this period that has "distinguished" Philadelphia. From their founding thirty-two years would pass before the Phils appeared in their first World Series in 1915, bowing to the Red Sox, despite the pitching of Grover Cleveland Alexander. Four of the five contests, all Boston victories, were decided by one run. Another thirty-five seasons would go by before Robin Roberts, Richie Ashburn, and the Whiz Kids of 1950 would make a second appearance in the fall finals. Similarly, in the Yankees sweep of these "Kids," a single run separated the two teams in three of the four games.

Unfortunately, those two seasons were more the exception than the rule. For instance, between 1938 and 1942, the Phils were the National League's resident cellar dwellers, averaging 107 losses per year, finishing anywhere from 43 to 62–1/2 games behind the league leaders. Despite the efforts of Richie (Dick) Allen and Jim Bunning in 1964, the Phils collapsed in historic and dramatic fashion, in part because of a ten-game losing streak in September. A look through the record books reveals that Philadelphia has finished last in their league or division thirty times, roughly one season in every four. In 1980, when the club finally did win their first (and so far only) World Series, ninety-seven years had passed from when the first Phils trotted onto the field. Now that is wandering on a biblical scale!

Chicago's White Sox got off to a rousing start, winning the first ever American League pennant in 1901. Five seasons later, they bested their crosstown rivals, the Cubs, to win the only all-Chicago World Series to date. Known as the Hitless Wonders, the 1906 edition of the Sox defeated a Cub team that set a major league record (since tied by the 2001 Seattle Mariners) with 116 victories during the regular season. In 1917, Shoeless Joe Jackson, Eddie Collins, and pitcher Red Faber helped give the pale hose their second World Series title. Unfortunately, in 1919, the White Sox's reputation was blackened when Jackson and others were thought to have thrown the Series against the Reds. Forty years (there's that number again) went by before the Go-go Sox of Nellie Fox, Luis Aparicio, Ted Kluszewski, Billy Pierce, and Early Wynn returned to center stage. Even with a clean reputation, the Sox fell to the Dodgers in six games.

It would be another forty-six years until the pale hose made it back to center stage. However, this time the outcome was much more to the south side of Chicago's liking. Backed by the bats of Jermaine Dye and Paul Konerko, the arms of Mark Buehrle, Jose Contreras, Freddy Garcia, and Jon Garland, and the leadership of Manager of the Year Ozzie Guillen, the Sox finally brought a World Series title back to the Windy City.

Those fans looking for signs as to why their teams haven't won the World Series in decades may feel that having the word "Sox" across the uniform could have something to do with it. White and Red Sox teams had played more than 174 seasons before celebrating their world championships. For that matter, being from Chicago might just be enough to put the kibosh on any postseason parties. Prior to the White Sox winning the Series in 2005, Cubs and Sox teams have endured over a combined 185 seasons without the ultimate victory.

Ah, the Red Sox. Today's fans might be surprised to learn that Boston, along with the Philadelphia A's, ruled the early American League. From 1912 through 1918, the rose hose were World Series Champions four times. In 1912, Tris Speaker and Smokey Joe Wood led the Bosox to the crown. In 1915, it was Speaker again along with righty Rube Foster and outfielders Harry Hooper and Duffy Lewis doing the honors. A year later, Hooper, Larry Gardner, and two pitchers, Ernie Shore and a fellow by the name of Babe Ruth, led the way. And in 1918, Ruth and Carl Mays each won two games as Boston took the Cubs, despite scoring only nine runs, in five games.

Then came "The Curse."

Once Babe Ruth was sold to the Yankees for the 1920 season, the Red Sox began to unravel. In the twelve seasons from 1922 to

1933, Boston finished last nine times and second to last twice. In 1931 when they finished in sixth place, they were still 45 games behind; in 1932 they lost 111 of 154 games and finished 64 games out of the running. Those Sox were red no doubt with embarrassment.

Come the 1940s, the Curse of the Bambino had lost some of its power, though not all. At least the team got to the Series. Yet Bobby Doerr, Dom DiMaggio, and Ted Williams were not enough to help Boston get past the Cardinals in the 1946 contest, falling in seven games. Cleveland kept the Sox from the Series two years later, winning a one game playoff at the end of the regular season. While in 1949, Boston led the Yankees by one game with two left to play, only to lose their final pair and another chance to play in October.

It wasn't until the magical year of 1967, after eight losing seasons, that New England enjoyed a classic fall. That was the season Carl Yastrzemski won the Triple Crown and the American League MVP Award, and Jim Lonborg bagged 22 victories and the Cy Young Award. Unfortunately, that was also the year they met Bob Gibson and the Cardinals in the Series, coming one game short of a world title. A similar fate met Boston in 1975, when they lost to the Cincinnati Big Red Machine, again in seven games, despite the home run heroics of Carlton Fisk and Bernie Carbo. And Sox fans still lament the day when Bucky Dent of the Yankees hit his infamous three-run home run in the 1978 playoff game that put New York in the Series and Boston in a funk.

As disappointing as all these outcomes were, none came close to the heartbreak of 1986. Leading the Mets three games to two, the Red Sox were one strike from a World Series title when a wild pitch allowed New York to tie the game. Moments later Boston first baseman Bill Buckner misplayed Mookie Wilson's ground ball allowing the Mets to win the game and tie the Series. Again the Red Sox had a chance in a decisive seventh game. Again they lost.

As you may be aware, all that changed in the fall classic of 2004. And a classic it was. The Red Sox were three outs away from an inglorious four-game sweep in the American League Championship Series at the hands of the Yankees, otherwise known as the Evil Empire. However, a Dave Roberts stolen base, of all things, sparked the rose hose to win four in a row against the Yanks to roar into the World Series against the St. Louis Cardinals. There, Boston won four more in a row to win their first world championship since Woodrow Wilson was president. Talk about (finally) answered prayers. No wonder the *Boston Herald* proclaimed, "Amen!"

Chicago's National League entry, the Cubs, lead the majors in patience. Much like Boston, the Cubs were a powerhouse in the game's early years. From 1906 through 1910, the Cubbies appeared in four World Series, including three in a row. In 1907–1908, pitchers Mordecai "Three Finger" Brown and Orval Overall and the lyrical infield of Tinker to Evers to Chance helped Chicago win back-to-back championships over Ty Cobb's Detroit Tigers. Those were heady times on the north side of Chi-town.

Franklin P. Adams, a columnist for the *New York Evening Mail*, committed the Cub infielders to baseball memory when he was asked to add eight lines to his column that was short. In July of 1910, Adams composed these now famous words:

> These are the saddest of possible words,
> Tinker to Evers to Chance
> Trio of bear cubs and fleeter than birds,
> Tinker to Evers to Chance
> Thoughtlessly pricking our gonfalon bubble,
> Making a Giant hit into a double.
> Words that are weighty with nothing but trouble
> Tinker to Evers to Chance.[2]

Looking back, though, one can now see how the 1906 Series against the crosstown rival White Sox planted the first seeds of frustration that were to plague the team in later years. That year the Cubs set a still-major league record of 116 victories in the regular season. Having led their league in batting, fielding, and pitching (with a team ERA of 1.76), the Cubs were heavily favored over a White Sox team known as the "Hitless Wonders." Yet with Ed Walsh hurling the Sox to two victories, the southsiders took the Series in six games.

Those seeds fully sprouted in the coming seasons. First, the 1910 Cubs were upended in October by the Philadelphia A's of Frank "Home Run" Baker, Chief Bender, and Jack Coombs, who in five games gave the A's their first world championship. Eight years later, the Cubs lost the Series in six games to the Red Sox, behind the arms of Babe Ruth and Carl Mays. Adding insult to injury, Chicago outscored their opponent 10–9 in the six games played. In 1929, the stock market wasn't the only thing that crashed. Despite a regular season that saw future Hall of Famers Hack Wilson and Rogers Hornsby drive in 159 and 149 runs respectively, the Cubs fell to the A's in five in that season's title round. In 1945, Chicago outhit Detroit 65–54, yet lost the Series in seven games to a Tiger team led by Hank Greenberg and pitcher Hal Newhouser.

Soon the Cubs hit bottom...literally. During the nineteen-year period from 1948 through 1966, Chicago finished last or second to last twelve times. Those dirty dozen seasons saw the team finish an average of thirty-four games out of first place.

Hope came to town in 1969, escorted by Messrs. Banks, Jenkins, Santo, and Williams. But she left in early September when the Cubs saw their 9–1/2 game lead of early August evaporate as the Miracle Mets surged to the National League pennant. By season's end, Chicago was eight games out.

Organized in 1870, the Cubs have represented the same city longer than any other franchise in major league history. From the great Chicago Fire of 1871 to the Cub meltdown of 1969, the club has faced more than its fair share of adversity. At times ridiculed, forever loved, Chicago has survived decades that would have caused lesser clubs to crumble and quit the game. Despite all their misfortune, the Cubbies have given their fans enough hope to persevere. In 1984, 1989, and again in 1998, Chicago made the playoffs only to fall short of their ultimate goal.

In 2003, baseball was poised for the most climatic World Series ever. Both the Red Sox and Cubs had advanced to their leagues' respective championship rounds. Both teams had come to within five outs of advancing to a fall classic. All baseball fans held their breath, hoping and praying that at long last one of them would be crowned champion again. Alas, it was not to be. The Florida Marlins overcame the Cubs as did the Yankees subdue the Red Sox.

It's a toss up as to which lyric best describes the Cubs attempt to return to the Promised Land: Paul McCartney's "The Long and Winding Road" or the Grateful Dead phrase, "What a long, strange trip it's been." True, Chicago has yet to surpass the ninety-seven years in the baseball wilderness of the Phillies, but they're closing fast. Yes, the Cubs have at least won a World Series, whereas teams such as Colorado and Texas have yet to even play in one. While the White Sox had to wait nearly ninety years for their 2005 World Series championship, at least they appeared in the fall classic in 1959. No team since 1945 has gone longer without making a World Series appearance than the Cubs. Nor has any team since 1908 waited longer to win a championship.

Fortunately, patience is a virtue.

God does answer our prayers in his own way, in his own time. We may petition our Father for assistance in conceiving a child, gaining employment, overcoming an illness. Often, things do not turn out as quickly as we had planned or as we had hoped. We urgently seek to have God fulfill our wishes; perhaps what we should do is take the time to consent to his. If we are not able to have children of our own, maybe we are meant to adopt. If we fail to land the job of our dreams, maybe there is another that better suits our talents.

Though we may be wandering in our personal wilderness, we are not alone. Isaiah said as much when he prophesied, *"Look, the young woman is with child and shall bear a son, and shall name him Immanuel"* (Isaiah 7:14). From Matthew (1:23) we learn that Immanuel means "God with us." Throughout the Exodus, God was ever present. He allowed Moses to part the waters so the Jews could escape the Egyptians. He provided manna to eat for forty years, and let water flow from a rock. In short, God gave his people hope for a better day.

While certainly not anywhere near a divine level, baseball in its own way provides its franchises and fans hope, even for those teams wandering in the wilderness. For the Phillies, hope appeared with the Whiz Kids and the National League East titles of the late 1970s before it was fully realized in the 1980 World Series. Boston's loyalty and patience was at long last rewarded in 2004, and the White Sox a year later. Even Cub fans' faith is renewed with each new playoff appearance by their beloved team.

Both the Bible and baseball teach us that comfort can be found in a season of despair. In the midst of their twenty-one-year interval between World Series dates, the Red Sox faithful could cheer Jackie Jensen, who captured the 1958 American League Most Valuable Player Award with his league leading 122 RBIs. Philadelphia's last place finish the same season was graced by Richie Ashburn's .350 average and accompanying batting title. Though Boston was 32 games out of first at the end of the 1960 season, Pete Runnels provided a ray of light for the rose hose with his league leading batting average. In spite of their team's collapse in 1964, Phillie fans could take solace in pitcher Jim Bunning's perfect game against the Pirates. Andre Dawson gave Cub fans reason to cheer in an otherwise dismal year. In 1987, his 49 home runs and 137 RBIs led the league and earned him the MVP despite a last-place finish by the team. And when the players' strike canceled their postseason hopes in 1994, White Sox disciples could point to the second of Frank Thomas' back-to-back MVP awards.

Just as Moses, Aaron, and Joshua provided leadership to the Jews during their journey, players step up to inspire teammates and fans alike. Each generation, each team has their own stars that shine bright. Look at the Red Sox. Ted Williams begat Carl Yastrzemski who begat Fred Lynn and Jim Rice who begat Manny Ramirez; Johnny Pesky begat Rico Petrocelli who begat Rick Burleson who begat Nomar Garciaparra; Jim Lonborg begat Luis Tiant who begat Roger Clemens who begat Pedro Martinez.

However, being chosen or being gifted is no guarantee of realizing our dream. As we've seen, Moses was selected by God to lead his Chosen People. He came face to face with "I AM" as the burning bush, brought down the Ten Commandments from Mount Sinai, parted the waters, and led the Jews out of Egypt to the Promised Land. Yet Moses never set foot there himself.

Similarly, Ferguson Jenkins never participated in the playoffs in his nineteen years as a player, despite pitching for four different teams. Fergie's idea of increasing his odds by playing for a number of clubs was sound; it's just that his uniforms bore the unfortunate names Phillies, Cubs, Rangers, and Red Sox.

All too often we become fixed on the journey's end and forget the journey itself. For Cub and Red Sox fans, they have been blessed to follow the trials and tribulations of their tribes within two of baseball's grandest cathedrals, Wrigley Field and Fenway Park. Mention the names of these ball parks to any fan of the game and images immediately come to mind: afternoon games among the sun-bleached, ivy-covered walls of Wrigley, the wind blowing out. Or grilled sausages along Yawkey Way, the Pesky pole, and the Green Monster of Fenway. Denizens of Chicago's north side and fans of the Fens have been privileged to see some of the greatest players of all time—from Wilson to Williams, Banks to Boggs, Fergie to the Rocket—grace the green, green grass of the home field. There, it's not whether you've won or lost, it's that you've seen a game.

Our time is not God's time, which is why God granted us patience, which is why he gave us prayer. We pray so that we may become closer to God, to understand as best we can his plan for us and our response to him. Our time is not baseball time, either. Which is why players and fans all across the country—whether they wear red socks or white, cheer for Cardinals or Blue Jays, or follow Angels or Devil Rays—place such faith in the rally cry, "Wait till next year!" Next year will come someday. It may be the birth of a son or daughter, or moving into a new home, or landing a better job. It may be a trip to the land of your ancestors, or finding a peacefulness in your heart. It may even be a World Series victory for the Cubs. Whenever next year comes, whatever next year brings, there will be songs of joy, tears of gratitude, and shouts of exultation.

Our wait will be over. Our wait will have been worth it.

Just ask Red Sox Nation.

"WITH ONE TOSS A SERIES WAS LOST, WITH ANOTHER A SERIES WON."

A tale of two pitches by New York Yankee Ralph Terry

"And on the third day he will be raised."

MATTHEW 20:19

TEACHING US FORGIVENESS was but one of many reasons that Jesus walked among humanity. He also taught us the value of good works. *Very truly, I tell you, the one who believes in me will also do the works that I do and, in fact, will do greater works than these…* (John 14:12).

Not only can we learn this lesson from the Bible, but we see it played out every season on a baseball diamond. Individually, if a player does good works with his bat, glove, and arm, he is rewarded in salary and awards. Alex Rodriguez's $252 million contract and Barry Bonds' seven MVPs easily come to mind. Should enough players do good works together, the team is rewarded with postseason success and fan support, the most recent example being the Chicago White Sox world championship. On a community level, if enough citizens do good works, we all reap the rewards of improved schools, increased funding for the arts, and more opportunities for the disadvantaged, maybe even a new state-of-the-art baseball stadium.

Yes, it sounds simple. Yet the combined notions of baseball, forgiveness, and good works help explain one of the most mysterious and glorious events in all of Christianity.

The Resurrection.

Forgiveness and good works were just warm-ups for the Lord's true purpose here on earth. Namely, to suffer, die, be buried, and rise again. In fact, Isaiah told the Jews what Christ was going to do long before it actually happened.

> *"Now I will arise," says the* LORD,
>   *"now I will lift myself up;*
>   *now I will be exalted"* (Isaiah 33:10).

Jesus himself foretold of his passion. Matthew, Mark, and Luke write about it in the gospels. It was that important.

He took the twelve aside again and began to tell them what was to happen to him, saying, "See, we are going up to Jerusalem, and the Son of Man will be handed over to the chief priests and the scribes, and they will condemn him to death; then they will hand him over to the Gentiles; they will mock him, and spit upon him, and flog him, and kill him; and after three days he will rise again" (Mark 10:32–34).

And so he was killed. And so he did rise.

But what was it like to be crucified? In that day and age, crucifixion was a standard form of execution performed by the Romans against enemies of the empire. Those sentenced were bound or nailed to a cross, hoisted up outside the city walls in the midday sun of the Middle East, and left to die of dehydration or asphyxiation. Sometimes legs or ribs were broken to hasten the process; a sword to the side was not uncommon. Death was slow. Death was painful.

In his book, *Death on a Friday Afternoon*, Richard John Neuhaus meditates on the last words of Jesus from the cross. From these seven thoughts, we learn everything we need to know about Jesus' mission on earth and ours.[1]

"Father, forgive them; for they do not know what they are doing" (Luke 23:34). Who are they? Those who condemned Jesus, those who mocked him, who crucified him, who failed to believe in him. Who are they? We are. Those of us who can't help but fail him through our anger, our selfishness, our envy, our lust, our humanness. Yet, even on the cross, Jesus forgave them then and forgives us now. And asks us to do the same.

Truly I tell you, today you will be with me in Paradise" (Luke 23:43). By his death and resurrection, Christ is leading us all home to God the Father, from the repentant thief at his side on the cross to the last one of us left standing on the planet.

"Woman, here is your son....Here is your mother" (John 19:26–27). Jesus was not just providing security for his mother, giving her a son in John, or even John a mother in Mary. No, it was more than that. Christ's mother is now our mother. We are her children. We are one another's sons and mothers, fathers and daughters, brothers and sisters.

"My God, my God, why have you forsaken me?" (Mark 15:34). Even in Christ's moment of desolation, in an apparent cry of abandonment, Jesus addressed God as *my* God. Said twice for emphasis. Though seemingly forsaken, said twice for affection.

"I am thirsty" (John 19:28). As we all thirst, so did Jesus for the comfort of his Father, for only God can truly quench our spiritual longing.

"It is finished" (John 19:30). Jesus said that it is finished, but not that it is over. Rather, his mission is complete. Fulfilled. Brought to perfection. With death, the stage is set to rise to the Father.

"Father, into your hands I commend my spirit" (Luke 23:46). When Jesus sought release in the Garden from his ordeal, he prayed

to his Father, *"Not my will, but yours be done."* Having consented to God's will, Jesus is now ready to be welcomed home by the Father. As we learn to do God's will in our own lives, we also prepare ourselves to be welcomed home by the Father.

Though painful and agonizing, dying was the easy part. Only when Christ rose from the dead did his disciples sense the wonder of it all, realize the miracle and mystery they had been a part of, believe without a doubt that the son of God had walked in their midst.

So what does it all mean for us? By listening to Christ's words from the cross we learn everything we need to know to be saved: forgive others, take care of one another, thirst for spiritual union, trust in God. By being blessed by the Lord's resurrection we are given the one thing we need to see us through our darkest days.

Hope.

Hope that despite all our fears and failures, our sins and trespasses, our human imperfections, we are forgiven. Hope that despite dreams unrealized, loves unrequited, plans disappointed, children lost, marriages torn, despite our bodies growing old and failing us, we too, through God's mercy and grace, can overcome sin, can overpower death.

Hope that there is, indeed, hope for us.

What's more, as the Bible provides us hope, remarkably so too does baseball. Hope abounds every spring when players, coaches, and fans alike look forward to a new season, with all errors and failed opportunities of the past erased, with renewed opportunity to reach the Promised Land. Hope abounds every game when Sheffield, Ortiz, or Guererro comes up with the winning run on base. Or when Rivera, Wagner, or Gagne comes in to shut the door. Hope abounds every inning when fans cross their fingers that Hunter, Cameron, or Jones will leap high against the center field wall and bring that long fly ball back into the park. Or that Renteria, Vizquel, or Jeter can reach that smash in the hole to start a 6-4-3 double play. Hope abounds in the off-season when the Mets trade for Carlos Delgado, the Blue Jays sign A. J. Burnett, or the Dodgers ink Rafael Furcal.

Resurrection gives us a chance at new life. Every day we die to God. It may be by ignoring a homeless person on the street, using a cross word with a loved one, an eruption of road rage, a fist thrown in anger, a marriage betrayed. Every day, we also have a chance to be born anew, to rise again, to live as Jesus taught us, to grow closer to God.

To be forgiven. To do good.

Baseball can offer a resurrection, an act of redemption almost every day. Bob Brenly makes four errors in a contest, then hits a game-winning homer. Mike McCormick, after an eleven-year career as a sub-.500 pitcher, wins the Cy Young Award. Ruben Sierra and Julio Franco reemerge in the majors long after their careers were deemed over. After an eighteen-month layoff, Tommy John comes back from never-before-performed surgery to lead the Dodgers and the Yankees to the World Series. Andres Galarraga, the Big Cat, overcomes cancer to prove he has lives to spare. Another cancer survivor, Eric Davis, rebounds to resume his career. Willie McCovey, thought to be washed up, wins the Comeback Player of the Year Award at age thirty-nine. A bust for the Rangers and White Sox, Sammy Sosa busts out his whooping stick with the Cubs, becoming the only player to ever hit 60 or more homers three times.

Baseball is not one game or a season, just as our life is not just what happens today or this year. Neither is it one stop along the way; both are an entire journey. All of us will be faced with trials of one sort or another. Sometimes we overcome our hurdles, sometimes we stumble and fall. All that God asks of us is that we do the best we can each and every time. With success comes rejoicing. We have the opportunity to learn from our failures and setbacks. Experience is a great teacher and it can help us prevail next time.

One of the most memorable stories of death and rebirth on the baseball diamond concerns two pitches thrown two years apart.

After six games of the 1960 World Series, the New York Yankees had outscored the Pittsburgh Pirates 46–17, yet each team had won three games. With the seventh game tied 9–9, Yankee right-hander Ralph Terry was brought in to pitch the bottom of the ninth against Pirate second baseman Bill Mazeroski. On Terry's second pitch Maz belted his now-famous home run over the left field wall, stunning the Yankees and giving the Bucs their first world championship in thirty-five years.

Fast forward to 1962. Game seven, Yanks versus the Giants. Nursing a 1–0 lead in the bottom of the ninth, Terry faced the ever-dangerous Willie McCovey with the tying run on third and winning tally on second. On Terry's second pitch, the ball screamed off McCovey's bat as if fired from a bazooka, only to land in the glove of Yankee second baseman Bobby Richardson.

Two pitches thrown two years apart. One pitch landed over the wall, the other in a fielder's glove. One represented death on the diamond, the other rebirth. It took Ralph Terry two years to overcome his "death" at the hands of the Pirates.

Jesus rose from the dead after three days. By conquering death, the Lord gave us the prospect of everlasting life.

Hope.

Baseball and the Bible provide a never-ending supply of this most valuable virtue. In a world plagued by threats of war, corporate greed, death, and disease, the Bible shows us how we should conduct our lives, and where comfort may be found. Every spring, baseball affords us all a clean slate, a new day, and renewed confidence with which to set forth for the Promised Land. If we falter, should we fail, we are given another chance next at bat, next inning, next game, next season. Should we sin against the Father, he too grants us as many "at bats" as we might need to bring us home, to join him in his heavenly home. When we sin, we die to God; when we're forgiven, when we do good, we are given new life.

Forever and ever.

As Jesus said, *"I am the resurrection and the life. Those who believe in me, even though they die, will live, and everyone who lives and believes in me will never die"* (John 11:25–26).

Or, in the words of Yogi Berra, "It ain't over 'til it's over!"[2]

Post-Game Show

IN THEIR BOOK *Baseball: An Illustrated History,* Geoffrey Ward and Ken Burns interviewed one of baseball's finest players and ambassadors, Buck O'Neil. The grandson of a slave and the son of a sawmill worker, O'Neil played for the Miami Giants, Shreveport Acme Giants, and Memphis Red Sox before joining the Kansas City Royals in 1938. He was a teammate of Satchel Paige, and counted Josh Gibson and Jackie Robinson among his friends. In 1962, he became the first African American to ever coach in the big leagues. Baseball was his life.

At the end of his interview, Mr. O'Neil was asked, "What has a lifetime of baseball taught you?" This is how Buck replied:

> It's a religion. For me. You understand? If you go by the rules, it is right. The things you *can* do. The things that you can't do, that you aren't supposed to do. And if these things are carried out, it makes for a beautiful picture overall. It's a very beautiful thing because it taught me and it teaches everyone to live by the rules, to abide by the rules. I think sports in general teach a guy humility. I can see a guy hit the ball out of the ballpark, or a grand slam home run to win a ball game, and that same guy can come up tomorrow in that situation and miss the ball and lose the ball game. It can bring you up here but don't get too damn cocky because tomorrow it can bring you down there. See? But one thing about it though, you know that there always will be a tomorrow. You got me today, but I'm coming back.[1]

Baseball. It's a religion. Death and rebirth. Strikeouts and home runs. There will always be a tomorrow. There will always be God's forgiveness. Hallelujah!

Notes

Warm-Ups

1. Bull Durham, Orion Pictures, 1988.

Top of the 1st

1. Ward, Geoffrey C., and Ken Burns. *Baseball: An Illustrated History*, Alfred A. Knopf, New York, 1994, p. 3.
2. Ward/Burns, p. 3.
3. Ibid.
4. Nemec, David, and Saul Wisnia. *Baseball: More Than 150 Years*, Publications International, Limited, Lincolnwood, Illinois, 1997, pp. 8–9.
5. Ward/Burns, p. 4.
6. Ibid.
7. Ibid.
8. Moyers, Bill. *Genesis: A Living Conversation*, Broadway Books, New York, 1996, p. 11.
9. Davis, Kenneth C. *Don't Know Much About the Bible, Everything You Need to Know About the Good Book but Never Learned*, Eagle Brook, New York, 1998, p. 46.

Bottom of the 1st

1. Berra, Yogi. *The Yogi Book*, Workman Publishing Company, Inc., New York, 1998, p. 88.
2. Ward/Burns, p. 6.
3. Ibid., p. 21.

4. Astor, Gerald. *The Baseball Hall of Fame 50th Anniversary Book*, The National Baseball Hall of Fame and Museum, Inc., the National Baseball Library (with essays by Roy Blount, Jr., Thomas Boswell, Robert Creamer, Ron Fimrite, Roger Kahn, Ed Linn, Robert Lipsyte, Shirley Povich, and George Vecsey), Prentice Hall Press, New York, 1988, p. 171.

Top of the 2nd

1. Ward/Burns, p. 374.
2. Ibid., p. 45.
3. Ibid., p. 139.
4. Ibid., p. 134.
5. Ibid.
6. Kinsella, W. P., *Shoeless Joe*, Ballantine Books, New York, 1982, p. 7.

Bottom of the 2nd

1. Ward/Burns, pp. 154–155.
2. Ibid., p. 165.
3. Ibid.
4. Ibid., p. 174.

Top of the 3rd

1. Simon, Paul. *Mrs. Robinson*, Columbia Records, 1968.
2. Moyers, p. 346.

Bottom of the 3rd

1. Ward/Burns, p. 233.
2. Astor, p. 172.

Top of the 4th

1. Ward/Burns, p. 300.
2. Astor, p. 215.
3. Ibid., pp. 214–215.
4. Ibid., p. 215.
5. Ward/Burns, p. 250.
6. *Total Baseball: The Official Encyclopedia of Major League Baseball*, fourth edition, edited by John Thorn and Pete Palmer with Michael Gershman, Viking, New York, 1995, p. 142.
7. Levy, Jane. *Sandy Koufax, A Lefty's Legacy*, HarperCollins, 2002, pp. 72–73.
8. Nemec/Wisnia, p. 219.
9. Ward/Burns, p. 301.
10. Nemec/Wisnia, p. 220.
11. Ward/Burns, p. 229.
12. Ibid., pp. 291–292.
13. Ibid., p. 291.
14. Davis, p. 331.
15. Ibid., p. 387.

Bottom of the 4th

1. Hodges, Russ. Play by play call, October 3, 1951, courtesy of Major League Baseball Properties, Inc.
2. *Webster's Encyclopedic Unabridged Dictionary of the English Language*, Gramercy Books, New York, 1996, p. 1227.
3. Ward/Burns, p. 404.
4. Nemec/Wisnia, p. 422.
5. Ward/Burns, p. 409.
6. Hodges.
7. Ward/Burns, p. 324.
8. Ibid., p. 287.

Top of the 5th

1. *Total Baseball*, fourth edition, p. 130.
2. Astor, p. 255.
3. Ward/Burns, p. 429.

Bottom of the 5th

1. Halberstam, David. *October 1964*, Villard Books, 1994, p. 134.
2. Ward/Burns, p. 382.
3. Ibid., p. 145.
4. Astor, p. 247.
5. Ibid., p. 250.

Top of the 6th

1. Astor, p. 274.
2. Ward/Burns, p. 84.
3. *Total Baseball: The Official Encyclopedia of Major League Baseball*, seventh edition, edited by John Thorn, Pete Palmer, and Michael Gershman with Matthew Silverman, Sean Lahman, and Greg Spira, Total Sports Publishing, New York, 2001, p. 2471.
4. Ibid., p. 2468.
5. *Total Baseball*, fourth edition, p. 127.
6. Astor, p. 141.
7. Ward/Burns, p. 370.
8. Astor, p. 301.
9. Ward/Burns, p. 425.

Top of the 7th

1. Berra, p. 9.
2. McMane, Fred. *Quotable Casey*, Towle House Publishing, Nashville, 2002, p. 48.

3. Ibid., p. 46.
4. Ibid., p. 42.
5. Ibid., p. 41.
6. Ibid., p. 22.
7. Ibid., p. 10.
8. Ibid., p. 56.
9. Ibid., p. 70.
10. Ibid., p. 12.
11. Ibid., p. 68.
12. Ibid., p. 64.
13. Ibid., p. 88.
14. Ibid., p. 82.
15. Ibid., p. 105.
16. Ibid., p. 102.
17. Ibid.
18. Ibid.
19. Ibid., p. 100.
20. Ibid., p. 107.
21. Ibid., p. 37.
22. Ibid., p. 33.
23. Ibid., p. 16.
24. Ibid., p. 53.
25. Ibid., p. 65.
26. Sterry, David, and Arielle Eckstut. *Satchel Sez*, Three Rivers Press, New York, 2001, p. 48.
27. Ibid., p. 82.
28. Ibid., p. 34.
29. Ibid., p. 48.
30. Ibid., p. 7.
31. McMane, p. 64.
32. Sterry and Eckstut, p. 34.
33. Ibid., p. 46.
34. Ibid., p. 33.
35. Ibid., p. 69.
36. Ibid., p. 23.
37. Ibid., p. 20.
38. Ibid., p. 62.
39. Ibid., p. 23.
40. McMane, p. 79.
41. Ibid., p. 87.
42. Berra, p. 48.
43. Ibid., p. 42.
44. Ibid., p. 30.
45. Ibid., pp. 26–27.
46. McMane, p. 21.
47. Sterry/Eckstut, p. 57.
48. McMane, p. 27.
49. Berra, p. 48.
50. Sterry/Eckstut, pp. 56–57.
51. McMane, p. 22.
52. Berra, p. 69.
53. McMane, p. 65.
54. Sterry/Eckstut, p. 56.
55. Berra, p. 13.
56. McMane, p. 65.

Bottom of the 7th

1. Goodwin, Doris Kearns. *Wait Till Next Year: A Memoir*, Simon & Schuster, New York, 1997, p. 107.
2. Goodwin, pp. 107–108.

Top of the 8th

1. Cashman, Terry. *Talkin' Baseball*, PKM Productions, 1981.
2. Goodwin, p. 66.
3. Astor, p. 237.
4. Ibid., p. 241.
5. McMane, p. 93.
6. Kahn, Roger. *The Boys of Summer*, Perennial Classics, 2000, p. 147.
7. Ibid., p. 379.

8. Kahn, Roger. *Memories of Summer, When Baseball Was an Art and Writing About It Was a Game*, Hyperion, New York, 1997, p. xviii.

Bottom of the 8th

1. "Thank You Masked Man: When Roseboro Needs His Dodger Friends Most, They Are There for Him," *Los Angeles Times*, July 1, 2002.
2. Plaschke.

Top of the 9th

1. *Sports Illustrated*, cover headline, November 4, 2002.
2. Astor, p. 49.

Bottom of the 9th

1. Neuhaus, Richard. *Death on a Friday Afternoon: Meditations on the Last Words of Jesus from the Cross*, Basic Books, 2000.
2. Berra, p. 121.

Post-Game Show

1. Ward/Burns, p. 231.

Sources and Permissions

Every effort has been made to locate and secure permission for the inclusion of all copyrighted material in this book. If any such acknowledgments have been inadvertently omitted, the publisher would appreciate receiving full information so that proper credit may be given in future editions.

Scripture references are taken from the New Revised Standard Version Bible, copyright 1989 by the Division of Christian Education of the National Council of Churches of Christ in the U.S.A. Used by permission. All rights reserved.

All baseball statistics come from Total Baseball: The Official Encyclopedia of Major League Baseball, seventh edition, edited by John Thorn, Pete Palmer, and Michael Gershman with Matthew Silverman, Sean Lahman, and Greg Spira, Total Sports Publishing, New York, 2001.

Yogi Berra quotes excerpted from The Yogi Book: I Really Didn't Say Everything I Said, copyright ©1998 by L.T.D. Enterprises. Used by permission of Workman Publishing Co., Inc., New York. All rights reserved.

Satchel Paige quotes and related material from Satchel Sez by David Sterry and Arielle Eckstut, copyright © 2001 by Arielle Eckstut and David Sterry. Used by permission of Three Rivers Press, a division of Random House, Inc.

Material from Death on a Friday Afternoon by Richard John Neuhaus, copyright © by Richard John Neuhaus. Reprinted by permission of Basic Books, a member of Perseus Books, L.L.C.

Certain Doris Kearns Goodwin quotes reprinted with the permission of Simon & Schuster Adult Publishing Group, from Wait Till Next Year: A Memoir by Doris Kearns Goodwin. Copyright © 1997 by Blithedale Productions, Inc. All rights reserved.

Russ Hodges call of Bobby Thomson home run, October 3, 1951: Major League Baseball® game reprint courtesy of Major League Baseball Properties, Inc.

Excerpt from Shoeless Joe by W. P. Kinsella, copyright © 1982 by W. P. Kinsella. Reprinted by permission of Houghton Mifflin Company. All rights reserved.

CPSIA information can be obtained at www.ICGtesting.com
Printed in the USA
LVOW11s2059200515

439206LV00001B/1/P